Cambridge Ele

Elements in Applied Social
edited by
Susan Clayton
College of Wooster, Ohio

EMPATHY AND CONCERN WITH NEGATIVE EVALUATION IN INTERGROUP RELATIONS

Implications for Designing Effective Interventions

Jacquie D. Vorauer
University of Manitoba, Canada

CAMBRIDGE
UNIVERSITY PRESS

CAMBRIDGE
UNIVERSITY PRESS

University Printing House, Cambridge CB2 8BS, United Kingdom

One Liberty Plaza, 20th Floor, New York, NY 10006, USA

477 Williamstown Road, Port Melbourne, VIC 3207, Australia

314–321, 3rd Floor, Plot 3, Splendor Forum, Jasola District Centre,
New Delhi – 110025, India

79 Anson Road, #06–04/06, Singapore 079906

Cambridge University Press is part of the University of Cambridge.

It furthers the University's mission by disseminating knowledge in the pursuit of
education, learning, and research at the highest international levels of excellence.

www.cambridge.org
Information on this title: www.cambridge.org/9781108713108
DOI: 10.1017/9781108614924

First published 2019

A catalogue record for this publication is available from the British Library.

ISBN 978-1-108-71310-8 Paperback
ISSN 2631-777X (Online)
ISSN 2631-7761 (Print)

Empathy and Concern with Negative Evaluation in Intergroup Relations

Implications for Designing Effective Interventions

Elements in Applied Social Psychology

DOI: 10.1017/9781108614924
First published online: February 2019

Jacquie D. Vorauer
University of Manitoba, Canada

Author for correspondence: Jacquie.Vorauer@umanitoba.ca

Abstract: Widespread belief in the benefits of empathy and its healing power is evident in public discourse and across diverse news and social media outlets around the world. Yet research reveals that empathy can sometimes have adverse effects on individuals' intergroup attitudes and behavior. A link between empathy and concerns with negative evaluation helps explain why empathy can backfire. Accordingly, using the minimization of evaluative concerns as an organizing principle, the author makes recommendations regarding when and how to encourage empathy in intergroup contexts, so that its potential to foster stronger social bonds across group boundaries can be fully realized.

Keywords: empathy, intergroup relations, intergroup interaction, concerns with evaluation, empathy interventions

ISBNs: 9781108713108 (PB), 9781108614924 (OC)
ISSNs: 2631-777X (online), ISSN 2631-7761 (print)

Contents

1 Introduction and Overview

Widespread belief in the benefits of empathy is evident in public discourse and across diverse news and social media outlets around the world. Its potential as a remedy for an array of societal and relational problems such as aggression, intergroup conflict, and discrimination has clearly captured our collective imagination. Indeed, a recent Google search on the term "empathy" and its variants yielded approximately 64 million hits (exceeding "self-esteem" at 63 million). Further along these lines, promoting empathy is a key component of many interventions designed to improve interpersonal and intergroup relations. These interventions are diverse in many ways. They include, for example, multicultural education provided to college students, mobile phone applications such as the Random Acts of Kindness (RAKi) app (see www .rakigame.com), visits to school classrooms by a parent and baby as in the Roots of Empathy program, and role-playing exercises in which students or employees are arbitrarily divided into groups based on eye color and given firsthand experience with discrimination (Elliott, 2017). Despite their different approaches, these interventions share in common a goal of enhancing individuals' empathy for other people.

At first blush, such faith in the power of empathy would not seem misplaced. Substantial empirical research does indeed document that it can have numerous benefits. Moreover, of particular relevance to intergroup relations, there is at the same time evidence of an "empathy gap" across group lines whereby individuals feel more empathic toward members of their own group than toward outgroup members (e.g., Bruneau, Cikara, & Saxe, 2017; Cikara, Bruneau, & Saxe, 2011; Gutsell & Inzlicht, 2012). The conclusion seems obvious: reduce intergroup conflict by promoting empathy toward outgroup members.

However, a growing body of empirical and theoretical work has revealed that empathy can sometimes backfire in intergroup contexts, exerting negative rather than positive effects on individuals' attitudes and behavior toward others. For example, it can lead individuals to defensively derogate outgroup members in response to perceiving that outgroup members are critical of them (Vorauer & Sasaki, 2009), detract from intimacy-building behavior exhibited during back-and-forth intergroup interaction (Vorauer, Martens, & Sasaki, 2009), foster selfish behavior (Epley, Caruso, & Bazerman, 2006), and increase revenge seeking (Okimoto & Wenzel, 2011). This research highlights the need for a measured approach to promoting empathy in intergroup contexts that is sensitive to the conditions under which negative outcomes are likely. Also evident is a need to identify strategies for circumventing such negative effects so that empathy's potential to foster stronger social bonds across group boundaries can be more fully realized.

In the analysis that follows, I first review research documenting positive and negative effects of empathy and then consider implications for intervention in intergroup contexts. My analysis and recommendations emphasize the potential counterproductive influence of concerns with negative evaluation by outgroup members, building on previous research and theorizing regarding empathy and evaluative concerns (e.g., Vorauer, 2013) to also consider how such concerns might be mitigated. Notably, I focus on the implications of different types of interventions for warmth- and positivity-relevant outcomes such as willingness to interact, feelings of hostility, and treatment of outgroup members. However, I also consider power-relevant outcomes of minority groups and other kinds of outcomes that are often an important goal of interventions, such as enhanced appreciation of the outgroup's collective narrative. Thus, I generally focus on micro-level (intrapersonal) and meso-level (interpersonal) rather than macro-level (social structural) phenomena (see, e.g., Wright, Mazziotta, & Tropp, 2017). I conclude by integrating the evaluative concerns perspective with other analyses of empathy that have been advanced, maintaining an emphasis on the intrapsychic and social dynamics instantiated by empathy in intergroup interaction contexts. The evaluative concerns framework is notable for its heuristic value and the structure it provides: considering the connection of empathy to concerns with negative evaluation provides an overarching, theoretically driven set of recommendations for when and how to encourage empathy in intergroup contexts that is grounded in individuals' fundamental concerns with social acceptance and approval.

2 Research on the Effects of Empathy in Intergroup Contexts

2.1 Definition

What is empathy? Given that there is considerable variability in how empathy is construed by researchers and laypeople alike (see, e.g., Bloom, 2017; Cuff et al., 2016), there is no simple answer to this question. For the purpose of the present analysis, I adopt a working definition of empathy as an other-focused emotional response involving an orientation toward 'feeling for' another person. Notably, according to this definition, empathy does not require an accurate read of the target person's feelings or directly experiencing the presumed emotional state of the target person, which is sometimes referred to as "parallel empathy" (Stephan & Finlay, 1999). Further, my definition is consistent with the one advanced by Batson and colleagues, namely, "an other-oriented emotional response congruent with another's perceived welfare" (Batson, Polycarpou et al., 1997, p. 105), which involves feelings such as tenderness when the other is suffering. However, I incorporate the term "orientation" in my definition to explicitly include *efforts* to connect and identify with another person's feelings, in addition to a more spontaneous emotional response, as the former also involves a benevolent stance toward another person's feelings. Empathy manipulations in experimental research typically involve instructing individuals to imagine how another person is feeling, and measures typically involve asking individuals about the extent to which they feel sympathetic, compassionate, warm, and so on toward another person (as in Batson, Polycarpou et al., 1997).

Perspective-taking is a related construct – typically viewed as more cognitive in nature – that involves efforts to imagine another person's point of view by mentally stepping into his or her shoes and seeing the world through his or her eyes. As with empathy, perspective taking does not necessarily involve more accurate judgments of targets: accuracy is but one of several potential outcomes of perspective taking efforts, and indeed recent research suggests that actively trying to adopt another person's perspective generally does not result in more accurate judgments about that person (Eyal, Steffel, & Epley, 2018).

Although empathy and perspective taking are conceptually distinct and can have different effects (e.g., Galinsky, Maddux et al., 2008; Gilin et al., 2013; Vorauer & Quesnel, 2016), in practice they are closely intertwined: perspective taking can lead to empathy (e.g., Coke, Batson, & McDavis, 1978; Vescio, Sechrist, & Paolucci, 2003) and empathy can lead to perspective taking (Vorauer & Sasaki, 2009). The overlapping nature of these constructs is further illustrated by the fact that in the research literature, perspective taking instructions are sometimes involved in empathy manipulations (e.g., Galinsky, Maddux et al., 2008), and instructions to focus on another's feelings are sometimes included in perspective-taking manipulations (e.g., Davis et al.,1996; Vescio et al., 2003). Accordingly, for the sake of comprehensiveness, I draw on perspective taking as well as empathy research in this review. I will not dwell on the distinction except where it is relevant to the outcomes being considered and when I discuss different types of perspective taking toward the end of my analysis.

2.2 Positive Effects

Before delving into a review of circumstances in which empathy has been shown to have negative effects, it is important to acknowledge that a large research literature documents that it can often have positive effects. In particular, empathy has been clearly linked to helping behavior; ample evidence also indicates that it can foster a sense of a bond with others in the form of self-other merging, whereby self and other overlap in individuals' hearts and minds (for more thorough reviews, see Batson, Ahmad, & Lishner, 2009; Galinsky, Ku, & Wang, 2005; Hodges, Clark, & Myers, 2011; Vorauer, 2013).

Especially relevant for the current analysis, a large number of studies suggest that empathy can have positive implications for intergroup relations. For example, in a now-classic study, Batson, Polycarpou et al. (1997) found that inducing individuals to feel empathy for a member of a stigmatized group (e.g., a homeless man or a woman with AIDS) led them to report more positive attitudes towards the stigmatized group as a whole (see also, e.g., Broockman & Kalla, 2016; Finlay & Stephan, 2000; Shih, Stotzer, & Gutiérrez, 2013). Similar effects have been documented in the context of conflictual intergroup relations. In one study, Pliskin et al. (2014, Study 1) found that Jewish Israelis who were induced to feel empathy toward a West Bank Palestinian boy through reading that he had been diagnosed with cancer reported greater support for conciliatory policies toward Palestinians in general, although this effect was limited to those with a leftist political orientation. In a similar vein, a correlational study indicated that Jewish Israelis' empathy toward Palestinians was negatively correlated with support for aggression as part of the Israeli-Palestinian war, with this relationship being particularly strong for those with a leftist political orientation (Pliskin et al., 2014, Study 5). Other investigations have also found a negative association between Jewish Israelis' empathy for Palestinians and support for aggressive policies and actions during the war in Gaza (Rosler, Cohen-Cohen, & Halperin, 2017).

Work by Galinsky, Todd, and colleagues extends these findings to implicit intergroup attitudes and a range of information-processing outcomes related to reliance on stereotypes (e.g., Galinsky & Moskowitz, 2000; Todd et al., 2011). For example, Todd, Galinsky, and Bodenhausen (2012) found that perspective taking enhanced individuals' recall of an outgroup member's stereotype-inconsistent behaviors and led them to make more internal attributions for such behaviors; perspective taking also enhanced their pursuit of stereotype-inconsistent information. Other research has demonstrated that empathy can enhance the perceived injustice of discrimination toward minority group members (Dovidio et al., 2004). Although effects are not always positive (e.g., Lai et al., 2014; Mooijman & Stern, 2016), results like these make empathy attractive as a tool for intervention.

Notably, however, studies documenting positive effects in the intergroup domain have typically involved abstract (and ambiguous) "absentee" targets who are not physically present and who are instead represented by a photograph, transcript, or video clip. Beyond not being well positioned to pin down cause and effect, correlational studies examining attitudes toward the outgroup as a whole also involve abstract targets who are not physically present. Moreover, where behaviors rather than attitudes have been examined, there have typically been clearly delineated response options whose desirability centers on warmth and is unequivocal. For example, individuals may be asked to sign a petition or vote in favor of allocating resources to an agency that helps an outgroup in need (e.g., Batson et al. 2002; Bruneau et al., 2017), be given an opportunity to directly contribute money to an outgroup cause (Bruneau et al., 2017), or be asked how they would respond to a hypothetical direct request for help from an outgroup member (Sierksma, Thijs, & Verkuyten, 2015). Many real-world circumstances in which it might seem worthwhile to encourage empathy are messier. Moreover, although it is also important to consider consequences for the experiences and power of those on the receiving end of empathy, these outcomes are often neglected in research.

Thus, research documenting positive effects of empathy has generally involved a restricted set of conditions and outcomes that do not always seem to correspond well to the types of contexts – involving conflictual intergroup interaction – in which it may at first blush seem most needed and desirable as an intervention. Indeed, much of the evidence of backfiring effects comes from studies involving the potential for evaluation, complex behavioral response options, outcomes relevant to target experience and power, or some combination of these. Ultimately, considering the experimental contexts in which positive versus negative effects have been demonstrated enables predictions about real-world contexts where empathy is more versus less likely to be beneficial. Such an analysis also points to how the likelihood of negative effects might be minimized.

2.3 Negative Effects: Contributing Factors

Evidence for negative outcomes comes from research involving ethnic groups that occupy different positions of power in society as well as from research involving other types of group memberships such as those based on university affiliation or experimental groups created in the laboratory. The negative effects of adopting an empathic mind-set that have been documented are diverse. In terms of empathizers' reactions, they include activation of negative beliefs about how the outgroup views the ingroup, negative evaluations of the outgroup, revenge seeking, and engaging in selfish and unethical behavior. For targets, negative effects can involve a reduced psychological sense of power. Under what conditions are such negative effects most likely?

2.3.1 Potential for Negative Evaluation

Individuals in conflict with members of another group may well be in direct contact with outgroup members and readily identifiable to them. In such cases, there is clear potential for them to be evaluated by outgroup members, meaning that outgroup members are in a position to form impressions and make judgments about them personally. Even outside of such circumstances, explicit reference to intergroup judgment or topics that lead individuals to imagine interacting with outgroup members can also raise the specter of evaluation. Moreover, because individuals are generally more sensitive to the possibility of negative than positive evaluation (Leary & Downs, 1995) and have a basic appreciation of people's tendency to be more favorable toward ingroup than outgroup members (i.e., ingroup bias), in intergroup contexts the potential for evaluation typically translates in individuals' minds into alertness to the possibility of negative evaluation in particular.

Regardless of how it is instantiated, the potential for negative evaluation is likely to interfere with the positive effects of empathy and make negative effects more likely. Why might this be? Unlike "abstract" empathy applied to physically removed targets, empathy adopted toward an outgroup member who is in a position to evaluate them is apt to activate individuals' fundamental concerns with social evaluation and acceptance and bring such concerns to the foreground of their attention. Because of individuals' basic egocentrism (Zuckerman et al., 1983) and motivation to know and manage whether they are accepted or rejected by others (Leary & Downs, 1995), when they try to step into an outgroup member's shoes and empathize and imagine his or her feelings, they are likely to become focused on gauging his or her thoughts and feelings about *them*. For example, if their own group is relatively advantaged, they might imagine criticism attached to historical injustice and wrongs perpetrated against the outgroup by their own group or resentment attached to ongoing discrimination and inequality. If their own group is relatively disadvantaged, they might imagine being disrespected or dehumanized by the outgroup. Even if there is no particular power differential, many of these concerns could still apply. More generally, in connection with any type of group membership, individuals may consider stereotype-based expectations that the outgroup may have about them. Although such a focus on negative possibilities may seem incongruent with the prosocial orientation associated with empathy, it is highly congruent with research in social psychology underscoring individuals' fundamental preoccupation with monitoring their social standing with others – and particular attention to the possibility of negative evaluation.

Much of the evidence for the moderating role of concern with evaluation is indirect, resting on a comparison across studies that show positive effects of empathy (which generally do not involve potential for evaluation) and studies that show negative effects (which generally do involve potential for evaluation). However, one especially relevant experiment by Vorauer and Sasaki (2009) was designed to directly test the moderating role of the potential for evaluation by an outgroup member. In this experiment, White Canadian university students (that is, Canadian students with a European ethnic background) exchanged written information about themselves with an ostensible partner in the study who was depicted as either White or Indigenous Canadian. Thus, when their ostensible partner was Indigenous, participants were in the position of potentially being evaluated by an outgroup member, whereas this was not the case when their ostensible partner was White. The written information involved describing their personal qualities and answering questions from Aron et al.'s (1997) closeness-inducing procedure (e.g., "If you could change anything about the way that you were raised, what would it be? Why?"). Halfway through the written exchange, participants viewed a segment of a documentary depicting hardships endured by Indigenous Canadians in Northern Manitoba (*Wrapped in Plastic: Housing Manitoba First Nations*). The segment focused on the abysmal living conditions experienced by an Indigenous woman and her family in a northern Manitoba community. This aspect of the study thus involved presenting all participants with an outgroup member who was physically removed and in no position to identify or evaluate them. Following Batson, Polycarpou et al. (1997), participants in the objective condition were instructed to remain objective and detached while viewing the documentary segment, whereas those in the empathic condition were instructed to imagine the woman's feelings. A manipulation check confirmed that those in the empathy condition felt more empathy and liking for the woman in the documentary than did those in the objective condition.

Consistent with predictions, the results indicated that when participants empathized with the Indigenous woman in the documentary in the midst of a personal exchange with an Indigenous person (i.e., empathy in intergroup interaction), they activated negative meta-stereotypes about how White Canadians are viewed by Indigenous Canadians (e.g., *prejudiced, cruel, unfair, selfish*): responses to meta-stereotype–relevant words in a lexical decision-making task were quicker in this condition than they were when the empathy toward the Indigenous woman in the documentary was enacted in the midst of an interaction with a fellow White Canadian or when participants adopted an objective stance toward the Indigenous woman in the documentary. There were no such effects on stereotype-irrelevant words (e.g., *dishonest, pessimistic*) that were also included in the lexical decision-making task. In addition, stereotypes about the outgroup (e.g., *lazy, irresponsible*) were activated when those low in public collective self-esteem, who generally considered their ingroup to be viewed relatively unfavorably, were prompted to empathize with the Indigenous woman in the documentary. Further, although either intergroup contact or empathy toward the outgroup alone had prejudice-reducing implications, the combination – empathy with an outgroup member in the context of an intergroup interaction – did not. Empathizing with the Indigenous woman in the documentary in the context of intergroup interaction also reduced higher-prejudice individuals' desire for future interaction with their Indigenous partner in the study and led them to perceive that their partner was less interested in future interaction with them.

Other studies in which negative effects have been obtained in the context of intergroup relations have also involved the potential for evaluation. Consider, for example, an intervention carried out over a year in a conflict zone (Eastern Democratic Republic of Congo) in the form of a talk show that encouraged taking outgroup members' perspectives (broadcast in connection with a radio soap opera). This intervention, involving approximately fifteen ethnic groups, was found to have a range of negative effects including less tolerance of a disliked group and less willingness to help them by giving them salt, a valued commodity (Paluck, 2010).

A set of studies by Tarrant, Calitri, and Weston (2012) exploring perspective taking in the context of university and national (British versus German) group membership provides a particularly interesting case. These authors used a perspective taking task frequently used by Galinsky, Todd, and colleagues involving describing, as if they were the outgroup member, a day in the life of an outgroup member depicted in a photograph (see, e.g., Galinsky & Moskowitz, 2000). Tarrant et al., who explicitly told their participants that the research focused on intergroup evaluation, found that those high in ingroup identification evaluated outgroup members more negatively if they had been prompted to take the outgroup's perspective than if they had not. Because Galinsky, Todd, and colleagues typically find positive effects and typically present the manipulation and (often implicit) measures to participants as unrelated judgment and decision-making tasks, it is tempting to conclude that the salience of intergroup evaluation helps account for the divergent results obtained. It also seems plausible that those higher in ingroup identification would be more sensitive to the possibility of criticism from other groups. However, as Tarrant et al. do not present data on underlying process and suggest a different account, this analysis is speculative.

Further evidence for backfiring comes from contexts that involve conflict or competition and where the other party's potential negative evaluation thus looms large. In terms of conflict, Okimoto and Wenzel (2011) found that when individuals were instructed to empathize with the feelings of someone who had purposefully treated them negatively, they were more rather than less likely to seek revenge against the person. Although this possibility was not assessed, it seems likely that these results were due in part to increased focus on the other's apparently negative evaluation of them, that is, more energy that individuals devoted to thinking about how they were disliked, disrespected, or disregarded by the other person.

In terms of competition, Epley, Caruso, and Bazerman (2006) found that when individuals were encouraged to take the perspective of members of another group with which their own group was competing, they activated theories regarding others' likely selfish inclinations that in turn made them behave more selfishly: Epley et al.'s results, which were obtained with temporary groups created within an experimental context, indicated that considering a competitive outgroup's perspective led individuals to think about that group's likely negative inclinations toward them and to then respond in kind. For example, in one study taking the perspective of members of another group increased individuals' belief that members of that group would exaggerate their need when seeking to draw on a common resource and in turn increased individuals' own efforts to draw on the resource. Pierce et al., (2013) obtained conceptually parallel results with respect to unethical behavior.

Two final points are of note here. First, as mentioned previously, in the context of intergroup relations, salient potential for evaluation typically means salient potential for negative evaluation in particular. However, as articulated in greater detail later, even when individuals imagine a more positive potential evaluation, as when the relationship is cooperative or individuals have favorable intergroup attitudes, positive effects of perspective taking have failed to materialize (as in Pierce et al., 2013) and negative effects have sometimes been documented (as in Vorauer, Martens, & Sasaki, 2009). Nonetheless, this analysis focuses on concerns about negative evaluation because such concerns are most apt to characterize contexts in which effective interventions are sought and because these concerns are apt to more reliably have harmful consequences.

Second, concerns with negative evaluation can interfere with empathic responsiveness in two key ways. One possibility is that efforts to empathize lead to thoughts about negative evaluation that preclude the experience of empathy and associated reactions such as self-other merging in the first place. In essence, the process is hijacked: instead of empathic feelings, other reactions such as defensive derogation ensue. However, it is also possible for feelings of empathy to coincide with different kinds of negative reactions such as discomfort, guilt, and a desire to avoid outgroup members (see, e.g., Vorauer & Sasaki, 2009). Although these reactions may not involve antipathy, they can nonetheless be highly problematic, as they have implications for the inclusion of outgroup members across diverse social and employment contexts. It may be easier and less stressful for individuals to restrict their interactions to ingroup members and thereby avoid the negative evaluations they imagine wherever they have the power to do this. Further, discomfort and inhibition may well be interpreted by outgroup members as reflective of antipathy (see Devine, Evett, & Vasquez-Suson, 1996). Both efforts to empathize and the actual experience of empathic feelings may thus have negative consequences as a function of concerns with being seen in an unfavorable light by outgroup members.

2.3.2 Complex Behavioral Response Options and Ambiguity

Intergroup exchanges are often complex and characterized by considerable ambiguity. In particular, direct contact in the form of face-to-face or even computer-mediated exchanges typically provides a broad range of behavioral response options: individuals could be passively or actively aggressive, try to be helpful, decide to directly refer to intergroup relations and issues or avoid such issues altogether, and so on. Moreover, considerable ambiguity can surround the appropriate interpretation of behavior. It can be unclear, for example, whether a remark reflects hostile or defensive intentions. Even see-mingly prosocial overtures such as providing help may come across to the recipients as controlling or patronizing instead of indicative of warm feelings or respect. Especially relevant to the present analysis, individuals may be uncertain about the signals their own behavior communicates to outgroup members. They may wonder, for example, whether making eye contact and asking questions will come across as attentive or aggressive, or whether being reserved will seem respectful or avoidant.

Yet in many research paradigms that have been used to study empathy, complexity and ambiguity are minimized by providing participants with clearly defined response options that fall along a continuum of presumed favorability – generally how much money is given to an outgroup in need, with no actual outgroup members being physically present in the moment. In such cases, a potential mechanism by which empathy can backfire is sidestepped. Specifically, because empathy is apt to orient individuals toward how they are coming across, it may fuel anxiety and concerns about the appropriate way to behave. When there is a diverse array of potential response options and a variety of possible interpretations, such anxiety can be paralyzing, detract from the clarity of individuals' outward behavior, and foster strained and awkward exchanges and miscommunication (Vorauer & Turpie, 2004).

The ambiguity inherent in such situations may also leave more room for egocentric bias in the form of transparency overestimation, whereby individuals see their behavior as reflecting their inner feelings more clearly than it actually does (Vorauer, 2005). Interestingly, this bias is one that is likely to be problematic even for those with more positive inclinations and expected evaluations: those with favorable feelings and intentions toward outgroup members may believe that their positive stance is more obvious in their behavior than it actually is, especially when they are feeling close to the target (Vorauer & Cameron, 2002) – which should be the case if they are engaging in empathy. Complacency about being understood may then detract from their communication efforts.

And indeed, in research where ambiguity surrounding response options has been maintained rather than minimized, negative effects of empathy have been documented even when expected evaluations by the outgroup are positive. In a series of four studies involving the potential for evaluation and also a diverse array of behavioral response options, Vorauer, Martens, and Sasaki (2009) examined how the intimacy-building behavior (e.g., positive other-directed remarks, responsiveness, self-disclosure) that White Canadians exhibited toward an Indigenous Canadian interaction partner was affected by whether they tried to take his or her perspective and empathize with their partner's feelings. Results across the four studies indicated that lower-prejudice White Canadians who engaged in perspective taking exhibited less intimacy-building behavior and left their Indigenous partner feeling less happy than did those who instead tried to remain objective!

The pattern of results across different comparison conditions suggested that the process underlying this surprising result centered on lower-prejudice individuals activating the meta-stereotype of their group (as a result of perspective taking) but expecting to be contrasted with it. These individuals believed that their Indigenous partner would see them as different from "most White people" (see also Vorauer, Main, & O'Connell, 1998) and view them in an especially positive light. Corollary measures collected by Vorauer, Martens, and Sasaki (2009) assessing the effort that individuals made to regulate their behavior help shed some light on how more positive meta-perceptions may lead to less positive behavior: for lower-prejudice individuals, the act of trying to imagine their outgroup partner's thoughts and feelings led to less self-regulatory effort, as reflected by enhanced performance on the Stroop color-naming task frequently used to index cognitive resource depletion (see, e.g., Richeson & Shelton, 2003). A picture thus emerges whereby perspective taking reinforces lower-prejudice individuals' confidence in coming across as sympathetic and tolerant and leads them to be complacent about working to communicate clearly – and to assume, for example, that their positive feelings are conveyed by subtle cues such as their nonverbal behaviors when in fact this is not the case.

Thus even when expected evaluations are positive, the effects of empathy can be negative, at least when implications for complex behavior in the ongoing stream of social interaction are considered. Consistent with substantial findings from research on basic social cognition indicating that individuals are likely to interpret ambiguous information in a manner consistent with their schemas and expectations (e.g., Darley & Gross, 1983), when the behavioral response is ambiguous, there is a great deal of room for individuals to "read in" signals according to the personal thoughts and feelings that are salient to them. Because any intervention that is broadly administered may also reach those with more positive inclinations toward outgroup members, it is important to consider potential negative implications such as these that may arise for individuals who are not necessarily the target of the intervention.

Notably, Vorauer, Martens, and Sasaki's (2009) research did also indicate positive effects of the perspective taking and empathy manipulations for higher-prejudice individuals' behavior, with evidence that these positive behavioral effects coincided with stronger self-regulatory effort and expected negative evaluation. It seems that activating the meta-stereotype as a result of perspective taking led higher-prejudice individuals to believe that they might be viewed in terms of that stereotype by their Indigenous interaction partner, and to then work to prevent this from happening. Although these positive results are in some ways encouraging, the fact that they were accompanied by expected negative evaluation and depletion suggests that if the option of avoiding the interaction had been available, higher-prejudice individuals may well have chosen this route. As well, because the participants in these studies were university students whose average prejudice levels were quite low, higher prejudice in this sample may more accurately be deemed moderately prejudiced. Those with more extreme negative attitudes than found in the typical university student sample may have more defensive and hostile reactions to expected negative evaluations by outgroup members.

2.3.3 Outcomes Relevant to Target Experience and Power

In much of the research documenting positive effects of empathy, the implications for absentee targets have been extrapolated from effects on empathizers' self-reported attitudes and helping decisions, with the assumption that more positive attitudes and helping by empathizers translate into positive outcomes for targets. However, whether this is actually the case is unclear. Beyond the general question of whether positive attitudes and helping decisions documented in laboratory settings actually translate into positive behavior toward outgroup members in the real world, questions surround how any such positive behavior will actually be received by outgroup members.

For example, research by Holoien and colleagues (Holoien, Libby, & Shelton, 2016) has highlighted that minority group members may react negatively to expressions of empathy for racial problems from White individuals, an effect that appears linked to the perceived presumptuousness of such reactions – that is, a perception that White individuals exaggerate their similarity of experience and ability to understand.

More broadly, another key point to consider is that extant research on empathy in intergroup contexts has generally focused on warmth-relevant outcomes, such as empathizers' helping and positive attitudes, rather than on power-relevant outcomes, such as the control that recipients are able to exert over valued resources and the extent they have a voice in decision making – outcomes that tend to be highly valued by members of minority groups and seen as even more important than being liked (see, e.g., Bergsieker, Shelton, & Richeson, 2010; Dixon et al., 2012; Nadler & Shnabel, 2015). Being the target of positive attitudes and helping may at best be irrelevant and at worst run contrary to the goal of empowerment. Specifically, because being on the receiving end of empathy and help from someone else may carry implications of dependency and neediness, the uncomfortable possibility arises that in some contexts encouraging empathy may serve to perpetuate group-based status and power differences. Along these lines, the results of several recent studies suggest that being on the receiving end of empathy from someone else can be disempowering.

Specifically, in a series of three experiments, Vorauer, Quesnel, and St. Germain (2016) manipulated whether one (White Canadian) member of an interacting dyad adopted an empathic or objective mind-set toward their (ethnic minority or White Canadian) interaction partner during a face-to-face discussion about topics such as academic and social experiences and social issues. Participants' scores on a variety of goal-directed cognition outcomes that have been shown to be connected to a psychological sense of power were then assessed. These included willingness to ask for more in a hypothetical negotiation and ability to exert executive control to maintain goal focus, as indicated by accuracy on incongruent trials of a majority-congruent Stroop task. The Stroop task required participants to indicate the color in which a word or letter string appeared; on the 24 incongruent trials, the color name appeared in a color other than its semantic meaning, whereas on the 96 congruent trials the color name appeared in a color that matched its semantic meaning. Accurate responses on the incongruent trials reflect better ability to remember, initiate, and act on the goal of reporting ink color even when most of the time reading the word provides the correct answer, and thus ability to maintain goal focus. Results indicated that being the target of empathy had a detrimental effect on participants' goal-directed cognition outcomes, whereas empathizers instead enjoyed a power boost. These effects were evident across both the intergroup and intragroup dyads.

How can such results be understood? There are two key processes (not necessarily incompatible with each other) that may help explain the effects of empathy on empathizers' and targets' psychological sense of power. First, according to the power script account, because empathy is typically directed "down" toward targets who are perceived to be disadvantaged or suffering in some way and in need of help and support, the solicitous stance that is inherent in empathy is intertwined with a power script that puts the empathizer in a higher power position relative to the target and affects each person's power-relevant outcomes accordingly. This account suggests that the target of empathy should be disempowered relative to the empathizer regardless of whether the empathizer is the dominant or minority group member.

Second, according to the meta-stereotype account, adopting an empathic stance activates group-based meta-stereotypes that contain information about how the outgroup views the ingroup: when individuals imagine an outgroup member's thoughts, feelings, and perspective, they access specific beliefs about intergroup evaluations and perceptions. For dominant group members, this meta-stereotype activation involves salience of a high-power group image, whereas for minority group members it involves salience of a low-power group image. Because the implications for individuals' power-relevant outcomes flow from salient thoughts about their ingroup's power, this means that the minority group member is disadvantaged by both adopting an empathic stance and being its target by virtue of activation of chronic group power differences.

Vorauer and Quesnel (2018) tested these accounts in subsequent investigations examining whether targets of empathy would be disempowered even when a minority group member empathized with a dominant group member. Their research followed the same basic design as the studies conducted by Vorauer et al. (2016), except that they also varied whether a dominant member empathized with a minority group member or vice versa. The results, although somewhat complex, were most consistent with the meta-stereotype account: the minority group member was disempowered by empathy regardless of who enacted it. That is, minority group members were worse off being the target of a dominant group member's empathy (versus objectivity) and were also disempowered by their own efforts to be empathic. Thus, empathy seemed to serve to exacerbate rather than mitigate chronic group-based power differences. By virtue of their chronic group-based power disadvantage, the reduced ability to effectively pursue goals and be agentic that accompanies a decreased sense of power would seem to constitute particularly unfortunate outcomes for minority group members.

2.3.4 Other Considerations

Of course the broader possibility remains that positive attitudes toward a group generated by empathy outside of interaction situations might have beneficial downstream implications such as a more favorable stance toward policies supportive of the target group or help directed toward the target group. Yet even here, there is the possibility of negative effects if the help and support provided are disempowering or dependency oriented (Halabi, Dovidio, & Nadler, 2016; Halabi & Nadler, 2017; Schneider et al., 1996). For example, Halabi et al. (2016) found that when Israeli Arabs imagined a situation in which an Israeli Jew offered help to an Israeli Arab, they perceived the assistance as a means of achieving dominance and reinforcing dependency more so than did Israeli Jews imagining such a situation. Schneider et al. (1996) found that when Black students received unsolicited help from a White student, they reported lower self-esteem than Black students who did not receive such help or White students who did or did not receive help from a White student.

A second key point to consider is that even setting aside concerns about power dynamics, implications of being the target of empathy for the favorability of targets' experience and attitudes are not necessarily positive. For example, results from analyses of corollary measures collected by Vorauer et al. (2016) and Vorauer and Petsnik (2018) suggest that although individuals may feel more positive and empathic toward targets when they try to be empathic (as opposed to objective), targets themselves do not report more positive feelings or detect that empathy has been directed toward them. The effects of being the target of empathy are not necessarily better when empathy is stated explicitly (as opposed to having to be inferred). In a set of studies, Nadler and Liviatan (2006) found that Israeli-Jewish individuals who were low in trust for Palestinians were more negative toward reconciliation between the groups when they were exposed to an expression of empathy from a Palestinian leader as compared to when they were not, presumably because the empathy expression was perceived as manipulative. The effects were in the opposite direction for those high in trust. Thus, the effects of expressed empathy were more negative for those who most needed reassurance – those low in trust. Relatedly, theorizing regarding intergroup apologies explains the finding that outgroup apologies do not necessarily lead to intergroup forgiveness in terms of low levels of trust that can lead to suspicion about motives and detract from perceptions of genuine remorse (see Hornsey & Wohl, 2013, for a review).

Before moving on to consider the implications of these findings and theoretical perspectives for intervention, a few final points are of note. First, additional theoretical analyses, not reviewed in depth here, have also pointed to potential negative effects of empathy. They are outside the scope of this review because they do not directly center on intergroup attitudes and behaviors but rather focus on broader considerations and other outcomes. In particular, Bloom (2017) highlights circumstances in which empathy can foster irrational or even immoral decision making, as when one identifiable victim is favored over many, and can motivate cruelty and aggression against those who might harm the target of empathy. Further, Galinsky and colleagues (e.g., Galinsky, Wang, & Ku, 2008) have demonstrated that individuals act in line with stereotypes about targets whose perspective they try to adopt, which depending on stereotype content can prompt negative (e.g., competitive) behavior.

Second, although individual differences are outside the scope of my analysis, they undoubtedly play a role. As noted earlier, levels of trust make a difference in how people respond to empathy. Of particular interest, individual-level factors such as chronic levels of dispositional empathy could conceivably guide receptiveness to intervention. However, although it may be tempting to predict that those higher in dispositional empathy might be more responsive to efforts to encourage empathy, some research suggests that it may be those lower in dispositional empathy who are more affected, at least when the empathy instantiation is a direct prompt and when the outcome in question is helping behavior (e.g., Davis, 1983). However, as this research did not involve interaction or intergroup relations and the results varied across dispositional empathy versus perspective taking, this intriguing issue awaits further analysis.

Third, it is worthwhile to consider generalizability of the negative effects that have been reviewed across different types of groups. Many of these studies – namely Nadler and Liviatan (2006), Paluck (2010), Vorauer and Quesnel (2016, 2018), Vorauer et al. (2016), Vorauer and Sasaki (2009), and Vorauer, Martens, and Sasaki (2009) – involved ethnic group membership. However, negative effects have been demonstrated for other types of group memberships as well. Specifically, in Tarrant et al. (2012), group membership centered on university and nationality, and Epley et al.'s (2006) studies involved experimentally assigned groups or student resident houses. Other work has documented negative effects at the individual level without reference to group membership (e.g., Okimoto & Wenzel, 2011; Pierce et al., 2013). According to the present analysis, negative effects are likely wherever the potential for evaluation is salient and especially when outcomes relevant to power are considered. The specific nature of the identities involved should be immaterial, although more negative expected evaluations should generally heighten the likelihood of negative effects. Thus, negative effects seem more likely across political party lines than across gender lines, although it is possible to imagine circumstances in which the opposite might be true (e.g., when sexual harassment is salient).

3 Implications for Intervention

A key theme of the foregoing analysis is that negative effects of empathy are most likely when there is the potential for evaluation by outgroup members, especially (but not only) when those expected evaluations are negative. Complex behavioral options also heighten the likelihood of negative effects and are also very much the norm outside of the lab – individuals are rarely as constrained in terms of the response options available to them as they are in lab environments. It also seems likely that empathy is generally contraindicated in any context where power-relevant outcomes of targets are a top priority.

Before proceeding to use this analysis to make suggestions as to how to enhance the efficacy of empathy-based interventions for improving inter-group relations, I briefly highlight some points to consider when evaluating the effectiveness of such interventions and the need to modify existing approaches.

Evaluating the Efficacy of Empathy Interventions: General Considerations

Although there are few systematic evaluations of the implications of "real-world" empathy-based interventions for intergroup relations in particular (see, e.g., Paluck, 2016; Paluck & Green, 2009; Stephan & Finlay, 1999), there is some evidence for the broad effectiveness of empathy training programs. Generally these programs involve instruction geared toward helping individuals recognize and understand others' affective states and improving their role-taking abilities, with varying emphasis on instilling affective, cognitive, and/or behavioral empathy. For example, one program administered to aggressive adolescent girls in four 1.5-hour sessions involved reacting to slide presentations of facial expressions, role-playing via playing charades and exchanging roles adopted in a drama, and imagining how the world would look from various perspectives such as that of a new grandparent (Pecukonis, 1990).

Stephan and Finlay (1999) reviewed numerous studies indicating that empathy training programs do increase empathy and can have other positive effects such as increasing self-esteem. More recently, in a large-scale investigation, Schonert-Reichl et al. (2012) documented that the "Roots of Empathy" program enhances prosocial behavior and reduces aggressive behavior exhibited by school-aged children, and a meta-analysis of 18 randomized controlled trials reported evidence for effectiveness of empathy training programs for increasing empathy (Teding van Berkhout & Malouff, 2016). Evaluations have also documented that social-emotional learning (SEL) programs in schools are effective in improving social-emotional competencies, conduct problems, and academic functioning (e.g., Malti et al., 2016). SEL programs seek to facilitate the development of competency in the areas of self-awareness, self-management, social awareness, relationship skills, and responsible decision making (Collaborative for Academic, Social and Emotional Learning [CASEL], 2003; see also Malti et al., 2016). Self- and social awareness competencies involve skills directly relevant to perspective taking and empathy.

In terms of points to consider when evaluating the strength of data such as these and recommending modifications, the first issue is that the question of how empathy affects outgroup targets or intergroup attitudes and behaviors is not addressed when the focal outcome of interest in an evaluation is general empathy or benefits to the empathizer such as self-esteem or improved academic performance. It is quite common for evaluations of empathy training and SEL programs to focus on these kinds of outcomes, as well as peer relations and behavioral problems, without specifically considering intergroup out-comes. Yet, to the extent that efforts to empathize with outgroup members are enhanced, the potential for backfiring in interaction situations remains, as does the potential for reinforcing group-based power differentials in such contexts. Further, recent analyses suggest that enhanced empathy for ingroup members in particular may have negative implications for intergroup relations. Bruneau et al. (2017) assessed "parochial empathy" or "intergroup empathy bias," defined as greater empathy for ingroup as compared to outgroup members, and found that it predicted negative long-term attitudes and behavior toward outgroup members across a variety of conflictual intergroup contexts – and was a better predictor than trait empathy. Based on these results, Bruneau et al. (2017) concluded that interventions designed to increase overall empathy in members of partisan groups may be ineffective for increasing intergroup harmony. Thus, there is the potential that empathy interventions may not have favorable implications for intergroup relations even when they do have other positive outcomes.

Second, interventions – whether broad in scope or focused on intergroup relations –tend to be multi-faceted, such that it is difficult to identify the role of empathy in particular in accounting for the effects on downstream outcomes such as behavior (see Stephan & Finlay, 1999, for additional discussion). Along these lines, research on the effects of the Roots of Empathy program has documented positive effects on prosocial behavior in the absence of effects on self-reported empathy (Schonert-Reichl et al., 2012). The mechanisms underlying the behavioral effects are thus unclear but could involve increased sense of social responsibility or salience of prosocial norms.

Third, the effects of short-term and long-term interventions may sometimes diverge, even when their basic elements are similar. In particular, it is possible that with repeated practice and rehearsal, empathic responses can become more automatic and internalized and therefore more beneficial. Although empathic mind-sets adopted purposefully in the moment may trigger conscious cognitive and affective machinations that bring evaluative con-cerns, power scripts, and meta-stereotypes into the foreground of individuals' minds, empathy that arises in a more natural, "bottom-up" fashion – because it has been routinized and internalized over time – may give rise to more truly other-focused reactions. As a function of operating outside of conscious awareness, automatic empathy may be less apt to trigger preoccupation with evaluation but may nonetheless activate prosocial behavioral scripts. This possibility, albeit purely speculative, supports the greatest optimism inasmuch as it suggests that even when there are immediate negative effects, more positive results may arise over the longer term.

The limited evidence for the efficacy of empathy-based intergroup interventions, together with the negative results often documented in experimental laboratory-based research, highlights a need for a nuanced and theoretically grounded approach to encouraging empathy in intergroup contexts. Using an evaluative concerns framework as an organizing principle, I first analyze when it is likely to be beneficial to directly promote empathy and when doing so is contraindicated, as well as how to potentially enhance the efficacy of empathy-focused interventions designed to improve intergroup relations. Next I use an evaluative concerns framework to consider the likely costs and benefits of more indirect approaches to encouraging empathy. My analysis is theoretical and highlights directions for future research.

3.1 When and How to Directly Promote Empathy: A Consideration of Context

The key idea that guides my analysis here is that in general, the greater the potential for negative evaluation by outgroup members, the greater the care that is necessary in encouraging empathy. I consider in turn contexts involving minimal, moderate, and high potential for negative evaluation, with different recommendations in each case. My analysis applies only to outcomes such as favorable attitudes and warm and friendly behavior toward outgroup members. When power-relevant outcomes of outgroup members are a priority, empathy is generally not advised: although it might not always be detrimental, there are no empirical grounds for expecting positive effects on targets' power outcomes in intergroup contexts. However, perspective taking may be more beneficial than empathy with respect to such outcomes, a point I consider at the end of this section. Recommendations are summarized in Table 1.

3.1.1 Minimal Potential for Negative Evaluation

When the perceived potential for negative evaluation is minimal, the path from empathy to more positive attitudes and behavior toward outgroup members is relatively straightforward and uncomplicated by the possibility of defensive reactions (Vorauer & Sasaki, 2009). When might this be the case? When groups are not in direct contact, as when aid is provided to outgroup members in a distant geographical location, individuals may feel anonymous to outgroup members and thus not be particularly focused on how they are viewed. Empathy clearly predicts prosocial actions toward targets in such situations. Even with less extreme distance, if individuals are prompted to empathize outside of immediate interaction and toward abstract targets, positive effects

Table 1 Summary of Recommendations Regarding Direct Empathy Encouragement.

	Potential for Negative Evaluation		
	Minimal	**Moderate**	**High**
Examples	Not Identifiable to Outgroup Members	Low Familiarity	High Conflict
		Limited Interaction Experience	Hostility
	Group Membership not Important to Identity		Aggression and Violence
	Children		
Directly Encourage Empathy?	Yes	With Enhancements	No: Promote Psychological Distance Instead

Note. These recommendations apply to cases where warmth- and positivity-relevant outcomes are a primary consideration. When power-relevant outcomes of minority group members are a primary consideration, empathy is generally contraindicated.

can be achieved. For example, Galinsky and Moskowitz (2000, Experiment 3) randomly assigned some participants to complete a perspective-taking task involving describing a day in the life of an outgroup member depicted in a photograph from the outgroup member's perspective, with group member-ship centering on artificial groups created in the experiment (overestimators and underestimators). Bias in individuals' relative evaluations of ingroup versus outgroup members, which was apparent in a variety of other experimental conditions, was eliminated in the perspective-taking condition (see also Todd et al., 2011).

Positive effects seem particularly likely for group memberships that are not central to individuals' identity. For example, in classic work by Batson, Polycarpou et al. (1997) prompting empathy toward murderers and AIDS victims, individuals were unlikely to have identities around being non-murderers or people without AIDS. In such cases, it seems less likely that individuals will have clear ideas about how they might be negatively viewed by outgroup members (here murderers and AIDS victims). However, as soon as identification is clearly in place, the stage is set for more negative effects, even outside of back-and-forth interaction. Recall, for example, that Tarrant et al. (2012) found that perspective taking led those high in ingroup identification to rate outgroup members more negatively, with only the prompt that the study focused on intergroup evaluation. No such effects were evident for those low in ingroup identification.

Although contexts involving low potential for evaluation are rare, due to the complex metacognition that is involved children may well be less likely than adults to become preoccupied with thoughts about how they are viewed when empathizing. Thus, empathy may prompt positive attitudes and behaviors toward outgroup members more readily for children than adults, which would seem to underscore the importance of early intervention for empathy-based approaches. The specific implication of the present analysis would be to encourage empathy with outgroup members in the age period before the development of a clear understanding of different perspectives on the self. Of particular relevance to the current context, some research and theory suggest that children's ability to see their ethnicity through the eyes of others can develop starting around ages 10 to 14 (Quintana, 1994, 1998), although even adults struggle with egocentrism in many circumstances (see, e.g., Kenny & DePaulo, 1993), and research on this specific aspect of cognitive development is sparse. Research on self-presentation suggests an earlier point of increased attention to others' views of self, around age 8 (Dutra et al., 2018; Shaw et al., 2014).

In sum, direct promotion of empathy seems apt to be broadly beneficial when there is minimal chance of individuals becoming focused on outgroup members' views of them, because they do not feel identifiable to outgroup members, important identities are not involved, or individuals are too young to readily entertain perspectives on themselves that diverge from their own.

3.1.2 Moderate Potential for Negative Evaluation

As soon as there is clear potential for negative evaluation, there is a good chance that empathy on its own will backfire. As articulated previously, by virtue of imagined criticism from outgroup members and concomitant discomfort or defensiveness, beneficial processes that can be triggered by empathy – such as enhanced self-other merging with outgroup members (Galinsky & Moskowitz, 2000) and perceived unfairness of discrimination directed toward outgroup members (Dovidio et al., 2004) – may fail to arise. Moreover, even if feelings of empathy arise in such circumstances, they are apt to coincide with other kinds of reactions such as discomfort, guilt, and a desire to avoid outgroup members that can have negative implications for intergroup interaction. It stands to reason then that if individuals' negative meta-perceptions about the way that they and their group are evaluated by the outgroup can be prevented or countered, more positive effects of empathy should be realized.

How might this be accomplished? When intergroup relations are not characterized by extreme hostility, taking steps to prompt open and direct communication at the same time as encouraging empathy may mitigate negative meta-perceptions and pave the way for empathy to be beneficial. Enhanced communication could be facilitated by encouraging individuals to adopt an orientation toward learning about and asking questions of outgroup members as well as by encouraging them to engage in more personal and direct self-disclosures. I now elaborate on the mechanisms through which engaging in each of these activities might enhance the positive effects of empathy.

Learning Orientation

There are a variety of reasons to expect an orientation toward learning about outgroup members to be helpful in many intergroup interaction contexts. Perhaps most important, research documents benefits of a learning orientation for outcomes such as reduced cognitive resource depletion and anxiety for both individuals involved in interaction (Leary et al., 1988; Sasaki & Vorauer, 2010; see also Ma-Kellams & Lerner, 2016). Such findings suggest that coupling the goal of being empathic with conscious efforts to ask questions of the target and learn about him or her might create a situation in which perceivers' attention is directed out toward the target rather than in toward themselves. That is, the other-focus involved in trying to learn about the outgroup member should defuse the empathizer's egocentrism and concerns with evaluation and lead them away from even thinking about how they are seen (see also Vorauer, Gagnon, & Sasaki, 2009). Learning orientations more broadly construed, involving a focus on opportunities for personal development and skill acquisition, are also likely to be beneficial in terms of diverting individuals away from a focus on how they themselves might be evaluated (Murphy, Richeson, & Molden, 2011), as is a promotion focus on approaching intergroup interaction as an opportunity to have an enjoyable dialogue with an outgroup member (Trawalter & Richeson, 2006).

A further way that a learning orientation could be helpful is via reducing the negativity of individuals' meta-perceptions regarding how they are viewed by outgroup members and regarding outgroup members' interest in contact and relationships. Considerable research indicates that individuals reliably overestimate how negatively other groups view their own group. For example, Krueger (1996) found that both Black and White Americans underestimated how positively their ingroup was viewed by the other group and Shelton and Richeson (2005) found that these same groups also underestimated their respective outgroup's interest in intergroup contact and friendship. To the extent that asking questions prompts clearer communications from outgroup members about their intergroup attitudes and perceptions, then, the information conveyed is likely to be more favorable than individuals' starting or "default" expectations. Social norms and self-presentation pressures guiding individuals away from communicating negative evaluations and toward putting their best foot forward should further enhance the positivity of evaluative disclosures in intergroup interaction settings (see, e.g., Blumberg, 1972; Dunn et al., 2007). In short, because actual intergroup evaluations by outgroup members are likely to be more positive than individuals expect – and outwardly expressed evaluations even more positive – anything that encourages more explicit communication of such evaluations should serve to temper negative meta-perceptions and thereby pave the way for empathy to exert a more positive effect. Moreover, research indicates that individuals who ask questions of interaction partners are better liked (Huang et al., 2017), presumably at least in part because they convey liking and interest in the other person when asking questions. Asking questions may thereby assuage the other person's evaluative concerns. Note that these mechanisms do not involve turning individuals' minds away from their own evaluation but rather reducing the negativity of their perceptions in this regard.

The notion that reduced bias and enhanced accuracy depend on the direct exchange of information rather than merely trying to imagine another's feelings is supported by recent work on "perspective getting" in the context of interpersonal interaction: Eyal et al. (2018) found that although mentally taking another's perspective did not increase individuals' accuracy in judging his or her emotions and attitudes, asking questions of the person did enhance accuracy. Thus, at the same time as empathy is encouraged, individuals might also be encouraged to seek understanding by asking questions and trying to learn about outgroup members directly rather than through their own imaginings. The pitfalls of overly negative meta-perceptions might therefore be avoided, such that empathy can have more positive effects.

There are some important additional considerations here. First, although there are norms that generally lead individuals to shy away from directly communicating or asking about interpersonal evaluations, in intergroup contexts efforts to learn about outgroup members' experiences and feelings may more readily yield evaluative disclosures because they can be framed at the group rather than the personal level. Second, research on negotiation processes suggests that direct encouragement from a third party – such as a camp facilitator, teacher, or perhaps even a mobile phone app – to ask questions and exchange information is likely needed: the mere opportunity to exchange information is not enough (e.g., Thompson, 1991). Third, although enhanced communication may on its own promote positive feelings and behavior, communication and efforts to empathize should together constitute a particularly potent combination. This possibility is directly in line with research examining responsiveness in close relationships highlighting that positive and responsive social behavior is enhanced by a combination of accurate understanding and empathic motivation more so than by either of these alone (Winczewski, Bowen, & Collins, 2016).

Self-Disclosure

Related to learning orientation but centering on sharing rather than asking, an alternative possibility is to stimulate communication by encouraging individuals to make more personal and direct self-disclosures. Such disclosures should accomplish the revelation of positive information in much the same way as asking questions but instead start the process with disclosures coming from the empathizer that are then likely to be reciprocated by the target. The potency of such reciprocity processes is underscored by research on negotiation dynamics. Two experiments by Thompson (1991) demonstrate that disclosures of interests and priorities by one party result in enhanced accuracy regarding what the other party wants and how much importance he or she attaches to different components of the deal on the table, as well as more beneficial agreements for all involved: in negotiation contexts, it just takes one person to take the leap of sharing or seeking information to trigger disclosures by other parties that ultimately improve everyone's outcomes. Also relevant here is research indicating that "perspective giving" – quite akin to self-disclosure, but specifically involving the disclosure of difficulties and challenges faced by ingroup members – is beneficial in intergroup contexts for the positivity of intergroup evaluations (Bruneau & Saxe, 2012).

A particularly fruitful path might involve encouraging explicit communications of empathy. In our lab, we have found that empathic feelings are not "transparent" to targets during intergroup interaction. In particular, a minority group member's estimate of a dominant group interaction partner's feelings of empathy toward him or her is not significantly correlated with the dominant group member's self-reported feelings (Vorauer, 2018). At the same time, research outside of the intergroup arena suggests that people respond very positively to the perception that someone else is taking their perspective and feels empathy toward them (Goldstein, Vezich, & Shapiro, 2014). Encouraging individuals to more directly express their efforts to empathize thus may be beneficial (see also Weisz & Zaki, 2017). Research by Holoien et al. (2016) cautions us though that – perhaps especially in the context of intergroup relations – such communications should not involve potentially presumptuous expressions of accurate understanding ("I know just how you feel"). Expressing interest and motivation to see an outgroup member's point of view is likely to be much more helpful (e.g., "I want to understand how this seems from your point of view").

General Considerations Regarding Empathy Enhancements

The "empathy enhancements" of encouraging a learning orientation and self-disclosure may increase both the likelihood that individuals will actually experience feelings of empathy and also that those feelings will result in positive responses (as opposed to, for example, discomfort and avoidance). They seem best suited to cases involving discomfort and unease stemming from low familiarity and limited experience interacting. This is because the suggested enhancements are based on the idea that negativity is overestimated and that direct disclosures of feelings and reactions will be more positive than anticipated. If intergroup tensions run high, individuals may well be unwilling to ask for or disclose sensitive information, and whatever information is disclosed may be quite negative or greeted with suspicion, such that the empathy enhancements backfire as well. A case in point is the aforementioned research in the context of Israeli-Palestinian relations indicating that expressions of empathy have negative effects when trust is low (Nadler & Liviatan, 2006).

It is important to note that although I have focused on the potential for increased communication and information exchange to reduce exaggerated negativity, these enhancements could also temper overly positive meta-perceptions when these arise, as Vorauer, Martens, and Sasaki (2009) found can happen for individuals with positive intergroup attitudes who engage in empathy in intergroup interaction. For example, increased communication suggesting insecurities on the part of an outgroup interaction partner could lead lower-prejudice individuals to realize that their positive feelings are not as obvious as they had assumed. Overall, then, counter-productive social perception biases in a number of directions may be reduced by the empathy enhancements I have identified involving seeking and sharing information.

A related issue that arises here centers on exactly what individuals should be prompted to ask about or disclose. Research by West et al. (2014), which demonstrated that discovering similarities with outgroup members on self-revealing attributes that are peripheral to the interaction reduces anxiety and increases interest in sustained intergroup contact, suggests benefits of encouraging the exchange of personal information irrelevant to intergroup relations. For example, West et al.'s research involved discovering similarity in answers to "would you rather" questions such as whether individuals would rather be extremely lucky or extremely smart, or never have anyone take them seriously or always have people think they are no fun. Given that individuals generally tend to underestimate similarity with outgroup members (Mallett, Wilson, & Gilbert, 2008), overall increased exchange of such information should enhance appreciation of personal similarities.

Remember, however, that encouraging empathy may well be counterproductive when power-relevant outcomes of minority group members are a primary consideration. By the same token, benefits of the empathy enhancements presented here are likely to center on warmth and positivity, as opposed to minority group members' power-relevant outcomes. Broaching more group-level topics, including points of intergroup tension such as group-based advantage and disadvantage, has the potential to better address power imbalances. However, because it raises the specter of negative intergroup evaluation such information exchange is almost certainly better combined with encouragement of mind-sets other than empathy.

3.1.3 High Potential for Negative Evaluation

At least from the current theoretical perspective, it seems unlikely that encouraging active efforts to empathize with outgroup members can be beneficial in the context of hostile relations, such as those involving aggression and violence. Indeed, when intergroup exchanges are highly threatening and involve extreme negativity, directly encouraging empathy is likely contraindicated. In such cases, there are significant obstacles to actually feeling empathy, including lack of motivation (see, e.g., Weisz & Zaki, 2017) – especially for those with a conservative political orientation (Hasson et al., 2018; Porat, Halperin, & Tamir, 2016) or inclined to glorify their ingroup (Berndsen, Thomas, & Pedersen, 2018). Moreover, highly unfavorable meta-stereotypes regarding intergroup evaluation are virtually certain to be activated and then lead individuals to form negative meta-perceptions about how they personally are likely to be viewed by specific outgroup members. One might think that in the context of a hostile intergroup relationship, individuals would be disinclined to care or even think about how they are viewed by outgroup members. However, to the contrary, in such situations perceived negative evaluations seem to serve to fan the flames of antipathy. Research by Kteily, Hodson, and Bruneau (2016) on meta-dehumanization is a case in point. Whereas dehumanization involves active and deliberate denial of outgroup members' humanity, meta-dehumanization involves perceiving that one's own group is dehumanized by an outgroup. Drawing on data collected in the context of several serious real-world conflicts, such as those involving Hungarians and the ethnic minority Roma or Israelis and Palestinians, Kteily et al. found that meta-dehumanization was an important predictor of dehumanization of the outgroup and aggression toward the outgroup.

In cases involving extreme hostility, it seems that a more beneficial mind-set to adopt is one that in many ways is the opposite of empathy. A growing literature illuminating how individuals can most effectively cope *intrapersonally* with their own negative life events and stressors points to an alternative approach that seems apt to have *interpersonal* benefits when applied in difficult intergroup exchanges. Specifically, adopting a self-distanced rather than a self-immersed perspective on negative experiences facilitates more adaptive coping (Grossmann & Kross, 2014; Kross & Ayduk, 2008), especially when coupled with a "why" (rather than "what") focus on emotions that facilitates abstract processing (Kross, Ayduk, & Mischel, 2005). A self-immersed perspective on a negative experience is typically instantiated with instructions to relive the experience as it if were happening again, whereas a self-distanced perspective is typically instantiated with instructions to "take a few steps back" and "move away" from the experience and essentially watch it from a distant third-person point of view (see Kross & Ayduk, 2008). Essentially, better outcomes ensue when individuals step back from their feelings and adopt an outside perspective on their experience, analyzing the reasons behind their feelings rather than immersing themselves in those feelings.

Research in this area has highlighted the benefits of adopting a distant, third-person perspective on events for short-circuiting counterproductive rumination processes and minimizing the extent and intensity of negative affect such as anger (Kross et al., 2005) and maintaining marital relationship quality over time (Finkel et al., 2013). It follows from this work that it may be helpful to encourage individuals to adopt the perspective of a detached outside observer on highly conflictual intergroup relations. Along these lines, in two experiments Halperin et al. (2013) found that encouraging individuals to engage in cognitive reappraisal prompted them to express less aggressive inclinations and a more conciliatory stance in the context of a tense intergroup conflict. Specifically, Israeli participants either completed a reappraisal exercise that involved viewing anger-inducing pictures and thinking about them in an analytic and detached manner or viewed the pictures without instructions about how to think about them; they then adopted the same mind-set when viewing an anger-inducing presentation about the Israeli-Palestinian conflict. Those in the reappraisal condition subsequently reported less anger toward Palestinians and more support for conciliatory political policies than did those in the control condition. Recent research conducted in the context of the Israeli-Palestinian conflict has further demonstrated that phrasing conflict-relevant policies in noun rather than verb form – and thereby promoting more abstraction and distance – results in less anger and more support for concessions (Idan et al., 2018). Adopting a more distant and detached mind-set may be useful not only outside of and prior to direct intergroup contact (see also Zaki & Cikara, 2015) but may also help down-regulate negative and destructive group-based emotions such as anger and fear in the heat of the moment, in the midst of intergroup interaction. Research on the generally disruptive effects of analyzing reasons for feelings – in terms of at least temporarily "unfreezing" affectively based attitudes and making them more amenable to change – further points to the potential benefits of an analytical mind-set when applied to negative intergroup attitudes (Wilson et al., 1989).

These various lines of research all may seem to suggest that perspective taking might be helpful even if empathy is not. However, by virtue of the negative contaminating influence of meta-stereotypes, adopting the perspective of an outgroup member is much less likely to mitigate hostile feelings than is adopting the perspective of a detached observer. That is, the particular perspective adopted is critical.

3.1.4 Power-Relevant Outcomes of Minority Targets: Empathy versus Perspective-Taking

As articulated in the previous sections, whereas encouraging empathy can be beneficial in terms of generating warmer intergroup attitudes and behavior in some circumstances, extant research suggests little optimism with respect to power-relevant outcomes of minority targets: empathy in the context of intergroup interaction generally seems to reinforce chronic group-based power differences. However, this is one case where the effects of perspective taking may be more positive than those of empathy.

In particular, the social scripts associated with empathy versus perspective taking are distinct in terms of the power dynamics that they connote: whereas people tend to empathize with others who are disadvantaged relative to themselves, perspective taking often involves lower-power individuals trying to take the perspective of higher-power individuals in an effort to better predict and manage how they are treated by someone with control over their outcomes. Indeed, Galinsky and colleagues have demonstrated that lower-power individuals are more apt to engage in perspective taking than are higher-power individuals (Galinsky et al., 2006). Thus, in the case of empathy the target is typically in a lower-power position, whereas in the case of perspective taking the target is typically in a higher-power position.

Accordingly, Vorauer and Quesnel (2016) reasoned that being the target of a dominant group member's perspective taking would be more empowering for ethnic minority group members than being the target of a dominant group member's empathy. Prior to a face-to-face interaction between dyads composed of one White and one Indigenous Canadian, the instructions given to the White Canadian participant were systematically varied. Those in the empathy condition received instructions based on Batson, Polycarpou et al. (1997) emphasizing that they should "try to imagine how the other participant feels about the events and experiences that he/she describes" and "try to feel the full impact of the experiences that he/she has had and how he/she feels as a result." Those in the perspective taking condition received instructions based on Vorauer and Sucharyna's (2013) "imagine-other" perspective-taking manipulation emphasizing that they should "concentrate on trying to get inside the other participant's head and on looking at the discussion through his/her eyes" and "imagine as clearly and vividly as possible what your reactions would be if you were the other participant, taking into account everything that you know about him/her and trying to adopt his/her own way of looking at things."

In line with predictions, results indicated that for Indigenous Canadians, interacting with a White Canadian who was trying to take their perspective left them with a perception that their group had higher power and status in society than did interacting with a White Canadian who was trying to empathize with them. There was no such effect in an intragroup control condition (in which pairs were composed of two White Canadians), and there were no effects of the manipulation on the positivity of individuals' meta-perceptions or feelings toward one another: meta-perceptions were generally more negative than actual impressions across both intergroup and intragroup pairs, with this effect being stronger in intergroup pairs. To the extent that enhancing minority group members' perceptions of their group's standing in society is an important goal, then, encouraging dominant group members to engage in perspective taking may be beneficial.

The question does arise here as to what might happen if perspective taking gives rise to empathy. A key possibility is that, congruent with the initial power dynamic that is implied by perspective taking, downstream empathy that arises from perspective-taking efforts in intergroup contexts may center on imagining the target's powerful and agentic emotions (e.g., anger) rather than those that imply a lack of control (e.g., feeling sad and discouraged), such that the implications for the target are not ultimately disempowering. However, this possibility has not undergone empirical testing and is thus speculative.

3.2 Indirect Approaches to Encouraging Empathy: Costs and Benefits

Many interventions designed to improve intergroup relations include empathy enhancement as a key goal but are based on providing specific experiences and information that will lead empathy to arise organically, in a "bottom-up" fashion, rather than on directly and explicitly encouraging individuals to empathize with outgroup members. I now use an evaluative concerns framework to consider the potential costs and benefits of different approaches of this nature.

I begin with the broadest, most general approaches and conclude with the most targeted and specific of the indirect strategies. Although there are potential problems to consider with each of the approaches, from an evaluative concern perspective the broader approaches hold more promise in terms of being least likely to foster and reinforce perceptions of being viewed negatively by outgroup members. My analysis of all approaches, in terms of their likelihood to foster concerns with negative evaluation, is summarized in Table 2.

Table 2 Summary of Strategies for Encouraging Empathy in Terms of Likelihood to Foster Concerns with Evaluation.

	Likelihood of Invoking Concerns with Negative Evaluation		
	Lower	**Moderate**	**Higher**
Strategies	Social-Emotional Learning Interventions with Children	Direct Empathy Prompts Intergroup Contact	Intergroup Dialogue Instructional Approaches (e.g., Role-Taking, Multicultural Education)
Additional Supports Needed?	No	Yes	Yes Contraindicated in High Hostility

3.2.1 General Social-Emotional Learning Interventions with Children

Given the aforementioned difficulties associated with encouraging adults to purposefully endeavor to empathize with outgroup members, approaches that involve both early intervention with young children and "back door" strategies that broadly promote emotional sensitivity and social bonds with others would seem to hold great promise, in that evaluative concerns are likely to be minimized. As discussed previously, concerns about evaluation are less likely to preoccupy young children because of the complex metacognition involved. In addition, focusing on connection with others in general may circumvent resistance and stereotypes (including meta-stereotypes) that would be activated by a focus on specific outgroups. This possibility is in line with research indicating that encouraging individuals to endorse incremental ("people can change") rather than entity ("people's traits and abilities are fixed and unchanging") implicit theories of personality development can reduce stereotyping and prejudice (Levy, Stroessner, & Dweck, 1998; Levy & Dweck, 1999) – and even enhance intergroup cooperation in the context of intractable conflict, as in research with Palestinian and Jewish-Israeli adolescents (Goldenberg et al., 2017) – without ever tackling stereotypes directly.

One recent example is the Random Acts of Kindness (RAKi) mobile phone app developed by Sara Konrath, which includes games involving activities such as identifying a character's emotions, determining how to stop a baby from crying, or helping an old woman cross the street. The Roots of Empathy program provides another illustrative example. This program seeks to foster empathy, social and emotional understanding, and prosocial behavior in schoolchildren through lessons and classroom discussions. As a central element of the program, a neighborhood infant and parent visit the classroom regularly so that children can learn about the baby's development and how to identify and understand the baby's feelings. Children also learn to identify and reflect on their own feelings and the curriculum generally emphasizes caring for others. As described earlier, a large-scale evaluation found that the program was successful in enhancing children's prosocial behavior and reducing their aggressive behavior (Schonert-Reichl et al., 2012); in general, many social-emotional learning programs have been shown to enhance empathy, emotional understanding, and prosocial behavior (Malti et al., 2016).

From an intergroup perspective, the key issue is whether the positive outcomes of such programs extend to include more positive treatment of outgroup members as well, a question that does not appear to have been directly addressed in research. Such generalization may seem reasonable enough to assume, especially as dispositional empathy is associated with lower prejudice (Bergh & Akrami, 2016; McFarland, 2010; Miklikowska, 2018). However, the studies by Bruneau and colleagues (2017) revealing that empathy felt toward ingroup members in particular is associated with *greater* negativity toward outgroup members would seem to highlight the importance of emphasizing inclusivity and focusing on superordinate identities. There is clear tension here between promoting generalization and potentially activating negative beliefs about intergroup evaluation. However, at least with younger children, it seems that incorporating an explicit focus on outgroup members could help ensure such generalization without strong risk of activating evaluative concerns.

3.2.2 Intergroup Contact

Despite a need for more research addressing the effects of intergroup contact on adults' racial or ethnic prejudice (see Paluck, Green, & Green, 2018), substantial research indicates that contact with outgroup members is generally associated with reductions in prejudice. A comprehensive meta-analysis conducted by Pettigrew and Tropp (2006) indicated that interacting with outgroup members leads to more positive intergroup attitudes irrespective of whether Allport's (1954) optimal conditions for contact (common goals, a cooperative environment, equal status for both groups, and authority support for contact) were met, although the positive effect of contact was stronger when these conditions were in place.

As with other indirect strategies, contact interventions may have positive effects through channels that do not involve empathy per se, such as humanizing outgroup members (Tropp & Barlow, 2018) or deprovincialization, which involves adopting a more complex and open-minded perspective on the ingroup and outgroup (Pettigrew, 1998). Nonetheless, feelings of empathy have been identified as a key mediating process in explaining these effects (see, e.g., Cehajic, Brown, & Castano, 2008; Pettigrew & Tropp, 2008; Tropp & Barlow, 2018). That is, contact has salutary effects on intergroup attitudes at least in part because it enhances empathy with outgroup members.

Even in the context of intractable conflict, evidence has been obtained for long-term positive effects of a peace camp intervention on both empathy and helping behavior (e.g., Malhotra & Liyanage, 2005). As with many contact-focused interventions, the peace camp program was multi-faceted, involving cultural activities, lectures, and discussions, as well as cohabitation for four days. A different example of a contact-based intervention that incorporates additional elements is the "jigsaw classroom," sometimes referred to as cooperative learning (see Paluck & Green, 2009). In this program, children from different ethnic backgrounds come together to work cooperatively on projects in which each person has a unique and important contribution to make: each contributes a piece of the puzzle that has to be put together for the project and understanding to be complete. Although the evidence for long-term generalized effects on intergroup attitudes is weaker than for positive impacts on immediate peer relationships (Paluck & Green, 2009; Roseth, Johnson, & Johnson, 2008; see also Bratt, 2008), evidence for reduced prejudice and increased empathy stemming from experiences in the classroom has been reported (e.g., Aronson & Bridgeman, 1979).

Notably, however, worries about negative evaluation can lead individuals to avoid intergroup contact when they have a choice about pursuing it (e.g., Shelton & Richeson, 2005), detract from the quality of their intergroup interaction experiences (e.g., Richeson & Trawalter, 2005; Greenland, Xenias, & Maio, 2017), and lead them to be self-focused rather than oriented toward making generalized inferences about the outgroup from positive contact (Vorauer, 2008). Indeed, experimental research has identified that, at least in part because of concerns with negative evaluation by outgroup members, intergroup interaction is frequently associated with stress (Richeson & Shelton, 2003) and miscommunication (e.g., Vorauer & Sakamoto, 2006, 2008).

MacInnis and Page-Gould (2015) wrestle with the apparent contradiction across research findings indicating positive effects of intergroup contact on the one hand and difficulties associated with intergroup interaction on the other, and they suggest that intergroup interaction experiences begin to have more positive effects once a certain level of contact (the "contact threshold") has been reached. According to their analysis, ensuring a greater number of intergroup interaction experiences – especially multiple experiences with the same outgroup member – and less time between interactions will allow individuals to reach the contact threshold sooner and thus set the stage for more positive effects of contact. Seemingly quite relatedly, other research has highlighted the importance of cross-group friendship development to improved intergroup attitudes and relations (Davies et al., 2011; Page-Gould, Mendoza-Denton, & Tropp, 2008; Paolini et al., 2004). Even "extended contact," whereby individuals simply know that another member of their ingroup has formed a friendship with an outgroup member, has been shown to reduce prejudice (Wright et al., 1997). Of particular relevance to the present analysis, the potential for one's own and others' cross-group friendships to mitigate concerns with evaluation and convey messages of acceptance and liking across group boundaries is likely critical to their potency (see, e.g., Shelton & Richeson, 2005).

Further along these lines, many interventions through entertainment media for which positive attitudinal effects have been documented can be construed as involving a form of extended contact (see Paluck & Green, 2009). Particularly important for the current analysis, the depiction of cross-group friendships – as in Cameron and Rutland (2006) where schoolchildren listened to stories about a close friendship between a child with disabilities and a child without disabilities – can communicate messages of cross-group acceptance and mitigate evaluative concerns. There can also be an opportunity for individuals to learn about different cultures in a nonthreatening way. Moreover, when individuals read books or watch movies about outgroup members and come to identify and form a social bond with outgroup characters, perspective taking and empathy should increase (see, e.g., Paluck, 2009).

Overall then, this work indicates that promoting intergroup contact in general and cross-group friendships in particular has the potential to both enhance empathy and reduce evaluative concerns in intergroup contexts. However, because concerns with evaluation constitute an obstacle to cross-group relationship initiation and development (Shelton & Richeson, 2005; Vorauer, 2005; Vorauer & Sakamoto, 2006), use of the empathy enhancements discussed previously – such as encouraging individuals to adopt an orientation toward learning about and asking questions of outgroup members – could help accelerate the formation of social bonds and help circumvent potential problems. Especially given that the negative effects of negative contact experiences can be more potent than positive effects of positive contact experiences (Paolini, Harwood, & Rubin, 2010) and individuals are highly reactive to perceived rejection and criticism in intergroup contexts (Hornsey & Esposo, 2009; Thürmer & McCrea, in press), incorporating such additional measures wherever possible seems well advised. Indeed, concerns about negative evaluation even appear to represent an obstacle to positive effects of imagined contact, with some research documenting a link from such concerns to backfiring effects (e.g., West & Greenland, 2016). Possibly such backfiring occurs because there is no actual information exchange to correct overly negative preconceptions and imaginings.

Such considerations and the need for additional supports seem especially relevant to contact initiatives and interventions implemented in the context of intractable conflicts, many of which also include an intergroup dialogue or conflict resolution component involving direct discussions of conflict, prejudice, and violence, such as the Seeds of Peace or Heart to Heart summer camp programs (see Martin, 2018). Otherwise, in light of the painful and divisive issues that are addressed, there is the potential for reinforcement of negative beliefs including meta-stereotypes.

Along these lines, although a recent comprehensive evaluation of the Seeds of Peace education initiative suggests significant long-term impacts in terms of subsequent peace-building activities of its graduates (Lazarus, 2015), some studies have found evidence that such programs can backfire and foster more negative attitudes in some groups (Ditlmann & Samii, 2016; Guffler & Wagner, 2017). Consider, further, Paluck's (2010) intervention, implemented in the eastern Democratic Republic of the Congo, where some individuals were exposed to a radio soap opera that encouraged conflict reduction in the context of a love story between two individuals with different ethnic backgrounds, and others were exposed to the soap opera and were also encouraged to have face-to-face discussions of the issues raised by the show. Those who were encouraged to have these discussions evidenced more negative attitudes and behavior toward disliked outgroup members at the end of the intervention compared to those who were not. Results such as these are directly suggestive of the need for additional supports such as prompts to adopt a learning orientation, to seek information by asking questions, and to express interest in outgroup members' point of view. In cases involving particularly sensitive discussions, it may be beneficial to move away from a focus on empathy and instead encourage individuals to adopt a distant third-person perspective during any dialogues that are encouraged.

3.2.3 Instructional Approaches

There are many different instructional approaches to improving intergroup relations (sometimes referred to as diversity or anti-bias training). They can involve, for example, education about other groups and cultures, direct and explicit discussions of group histories and experiences, cognitive retraining to increase differentiation of outgroup members or reduce stereotyping, and role-playing exercises. I focus here on approaches in which enhanced empathy is thought to play an important role, namely role-playing and multicultural education.

Role-Taking

First consider role-taking interventions. Some of these involve giving individuals direct experience with another person's situation. For example, medical students may undergo hospitalization as patients, which can enhance their appreciation of the need to improve human aspects of hospitalization experience (e.g., Wilkes, Milgrom, & Hoffman, 2002). In one of the older experimental investigations involving role-taking, Clore and Jeffery (1972) found that participants who traveled campus in a wheelchair for an hour had more positive attitudes toward individuals with disabilities, as assessed by a disguised measure administered four months later than did those in a no-experience control condition. Notably, these researchers focused on enhanced empathy as a key process potentially underlying this positive effect (see also Madera, Neal, & Dawson, 2011). Possibly the most well-known intergroup role-taking intervention is Jane Elliott's blue eyes/brown eyes simulation, in which students or employees are arbitrarily divided into groups based on eye color and exposed to negative group-based treatment to give them firsthand experience with discrimination (Elliott, 2017; Peters, 1971).

Along with the potential benefits of such interventions comes the potential for backfiring under some conditions. One possibility is that the end result may be more biased perceptions rather than more accurate understanding, as when differences between temporary versus chronic experiences are not fully appreciated: Silverman, Gwinn, and Van Boven (2015) found that as a function of projecting from the difficulties that they themselves experienced and not taking into account adaptations that occur over time, individuals who had a simulated experience with blindness judged blind people as less capable than did those in a control condition. More relevant to concerns with evaluation, as with intergroup dialogues there is the potential here for enhancing individuals' perceptions that their group is viewed negatively by the outgroup, which could prompt defensiveness and a desire to avoid intergroup contact. That is, as much as such experiences have the potential to generate profound insights and awareness, an emphasis on the culpability of one's ingroup for discriminatory behavior may contribute to negative meta-stereotypes and social identity threat and thus be counterproductive.

If knowledge and understanding are to be acquired with minimal negative side effects of this nature, ensuring that empathy enhancements such as an orientation toward learning and asking questions are in place seems critical. Indeed, in an evaluation of the blue eyes/brown eyes exercise, Stewart et al. (2003) found somewhat mixed results. There was evidence for prejudice reduction as assessed in terms of scores on the social distance scale (Bogardus, 1947) but not in terms of scores on the modern racism scale (McConahay et al., 1981). Stewart et al. (2003) also documented that in comparison with the control group, individuals who had done the exercise reported more anger with themselves, noting that such feelings could potentially foster defensive or aggressive reactions in the absence of additional supports. More direct evidence for backfiring was obtained in research conducted in the context of international relations: Trost, Cialdini, and Maass (1989) found that role-playing Soviet advisors in a nuclear war education game increased rather than decreased US participants' negativity toward the Soviet Union.

Capitalizing on technological advances, recent experiments have probed the effects of role-playing instantiated through embodying an outgroup member in immersive virtual environments. A number of studies have indicated that occupying an outgroup body in a virtual environment reduces implicit bias (see Maister et al., 2015). Further along these lines, although the results were not especially strong, in one study Oh et al. (2016) found that embodying an outgroup member (an older person) while trying to take his or her perspective had some positive implications for general reactions to the elderly. However, studies that have included an intergroup interaction element have yielded more negative results. For example, in a second study by Oh et al. (2016) that incorporated a threatening intergroup interaction experience, there was no evidence for positive effects. In another study that also incorporated a somewhat threatening intergroup interaction experience (a job interview), Groom, Bailenson, and Nass (2009) found that the combination of outgroup embodiment and perspective taking resulted in greater implicit racial bias. The need for additional supports when interaction settings are involved seems clear.

Interestingly, in a separate line of research, orienting members of a stigmatized group toward another group's experiences of discrimination has proved to be beneficial only when accompanied by a sense of shared experience (see Cortland et al., 2017). Possibly an emphasis on shared aspects of experience might sometimes constitute an additional important empathy enhancement in the context of role-playing. In particular, it could help divert individuals away from a focus specifically on how their own group might be viewed in a critical light toward analyzing the intergroup relationship from a more distant, detached, and analytical perspective.

Especially in the context of intractable conflict, role-playing may be only one element of a multi-faceted intervention (e.g., Shechtman & Tanus, 2006). Such interventions sometimes incorporate a goal of helping individuals attain a deeper understanding and appreciation of the outgroup's collective narrative and accepting its validity. As noted by Salomon (2004), numerous obstacles to achieving this goal need to be addressed. An additional obstacle highlighted by the present analysis is that greater appreciation of an outgroup's collective narrative may foster meta-stereotypes that are more negative, detailed, and salient and are perceived to be more accurate and justified. An uncomfortable or even painful reckoning with the responsibility that may lie with oneself and one's group for an outgroup's suffering may well be a step on the path to a more enlightened worldview. However, given the threat that is involved, this would seem to be a case where encouraging a more distant, detached, and analytical outside perspective rather than empathy and role-taking would be advisable.

Multicultural Education

Although the term "multicultural education" is used to refer to a diverse range of programs and initiatives (Sleeter & Grant, 1987), students in these programs generally learn about different groups in their society through reading materials, video presentations, and exercises (see Stephan & Finlay, 1999). For example, students may view a documentary such as *True Colors*, which depicts how two men, one Black and one White, are treated differently as they engage in activities such as looking for a job or apartment (Pearce & Ross, 1991) or be exposed to personal narratives from individuals who have "unlearned" racism (see Garriott, Reiter, & Brownfield, 2016).

These programs, which generally have a clear anti-racism theme, focus on educating students about prejudice and discrimination and enhancing their awareness of the benefits and advantages enjoyed by privileged groups in society. Studies involving predominantly White college student samples such as those conducted by Case (2007), Garriott et al. (2016), Kernahan and Davis (2010), and Soble, Spanierman, and Liao (2011) provide evidence that such interventions – whether they involve an entire course on diversity (Case, 2007) or a 15- to 20-minute intervention (Garriott et al., 2016) – increase awareness of racism and White privilege. Although empathy is not always assessed directly, it can be expected to accompany enhanced awareness, a relationship that has been demonstrated empirically (Spanierman & Heppner, 2004).

Notably, all of these studies also documented an increase in White guilt. Although increased guilt could conceivably be a step on the path to increased feelings of personal responsibility and motivation for social change, it likely also fuels individuals' evaluative concerns: an enhanced appreciation of the unfair advantages their ingroup enjoys and discriminatory behavior enacted by fellow ingroup members would seem to readily connect to expectations of resentment and critical evaluations by outgroup members. The implications for individuals' intergroup attitudes and behavior and openness to intergroup contact may thus be negative. And indeed, Soble et al. (2011), while documenting enhanced racial awareness, guilt, and empathy, found no effects on prejudice. Further, alongside of greater awareness of White privilege and increased White guilt, Case (2007) found a reduction in cross-group friendships, greater fear of other races, and increased prejudice toward some groups. Reviews of this literature have generally pointed to the conclusion that multicultural education programs are largely ineffective at reducing prejudice and discrimination (Bigler, 1999; see also Paluck & Green, 2009).

Yet there are some more hopeful examples. In particular, although Kernahan and Davis (2010) did not find any effects of a diversity course on individuals' reports of their comfort during or frequency of intergroup interaction immediately at the end of the course, positive effects were evident one year later. There is some ambiguity here due to the absence of necessary control conditions, but conceivably, somewhat consistent with MacInnis and Page-Gould's (2015) arguments regarding the importance of accumulated experience, these results reflect that the knowledge gained has the potential to stimulate positive change when coupled with concrete experience with outgroup members. Incorporating empathy enhancements such as an orientation toward learning about outgroup members and asking questions may facilitate this process. Of course, increased awareness and knowledge are valuable end goals in their own right. However, to also foster more positive intergroup attitudes and interaction, taking additional steps to reduce the potential influence of evaluative concerns may be helpful.

Further along these lines, experimental work on effects of salient multicultural ideology suggests that simply getting individuals to think about the core tenets of multiculturalism and how it can benefit society can prompt both dominant and minority group members to adopt an other-focused learning orientation and make more positive other-directed comments toward an outgroup interaction partner (Vorauer, Gagnon, & Sasaki, 2009), at least outside of high-threat situations (Vorauer & Sasaki, 2011). Specifically, in the research by Vorauer, Gagnon, and Sasaki (2009), some White and Indigenous Canadians read a passage about multiculturalism before intergroup interaction, whereas others did not. The passage emphasized that "different cultural groups bring different perspectives to life, providing a richness in food, dress, music, art, styles of interaction, and problem solving strategies" and that "each ethnic group within Canada can contribute in its own unique way" (p. 840). The passage went on to note the importance of understanding both similarities and differences among ethnic groups. Participants in other experimental conditions were exposed instead to anti-racist or color-blind ideology. Only exposure to the multicultural ideology was reliably associated with positive effects. Further, with respect to the consequences of emphasizing anti-racism or color-blindness, other research has probed the effects of merely completing the Implicit Association Test (IAT; Greenwald, McGhee, & Schwartz, 1998), an experience that tends to heighten individuals' attention to their own potential for harboring negative implicit attitudes toward outgroup members. These studies revealed that the experience of even just being tested for bias (i.e., without any feedback) led White Canadians to behave in a way that made Indigenous Canadians with whom they subsequently interacted feel less positively regarded (Vorauer, 2012). These results suggest that, at least in the immediate term and without additional supports, being alerted to the possibility of their own hidden biases may have negative rather than positive implications for how individuals behave toward outgroup members during face-to-face intergroup interaction.

Other research from our laboratory further indicates that exposure to multicultural ideology is empowering for ethnic minority group members, at least in part because it leads them to believe that they are making unique and valuable contributions to society (Vorauer & Quesnel, 2017b). Relatedly, exposing ethnic minority group members to multicultural ideology enhances their ability to persuade dominant group interaction partners of their point of view on contentious social issues (Vorauer & Quesnel, 2017a). Results such as these suggest that multicultural education programs might have more salutary effects on intergroup attitudes and interaction behavior, as well as on minority group members' power-relevant outcomes, if they stressed multicultural ideology more than anti-racism. Interestingly, research documenting a reciprocal link between multiculturalism and perspective taking (Todd & Galinsky, 2012) further suggests that it might be quite productive to combine a focus on multicultural ideology with empathy encouraged by other program elements. At the same time, research indicating that salient multiculturalism can trigger hostility in conditions involving threat (Correll, Park, & Smith, 2008; Vorauer & Sasaki, 2011) highlight that this approach would very likely be counterproductive in the context of tense conflict – especially as empathy is also contraindicated in the context of extremely hostile relations.

In sum, these indirect approaches to fostering empathy vary with respect to how likely they are to evoke concerns with negative evaluation, with social-emotional learning and interventions with children being least likely to focus individuals on potential negative evaluations by outgroup members, and contact interventions that also incorporate some form of intergroup dialogue and instructional approaches in general being most likely to enhance evaluative concerns. If one of the latter approaches is adopted, additional supports are likely necessary for positive effects to be realized. As with direct approaches, in the case of intractable conflict and high hostility, efforts to stimulate empathy even indirectly are likely ill advised, especially for approaches associated with higher evaluative concerns. Greater psychological distance is instead more apt to be beneficial in such cases.

4 Related Constructs

Empathy is but one of numerous overlapping and interrelated mind-sets that could be directly or indirectly encouraged in intergroup interventions.

4.1 Perspective-Taking

Perspective-taking in particular can be an antecedent or consequence of empathy and in many cases has parallel effects. As noted previously, one key point of differentiation centers on implications for targets' power-relevant outcomes, with perspective taking having greater potential for empowering rather than disempowering targets.

Several lines of research and theorizing further suggest that imagine-self perspective taking is apt to have more beneficial consequences than imagine-other perspective taking in intergroup contexts. When individuals engage in imagine-self perspective taking, they think about how they would feel if they were in the target's place, whereas when they engage in imagine-other perspective taking, they think about how the target feels (Batson, Early, & Salvarani, 1997), which could involve taking into account his or her own distinct characteristics and previous experiences (see also Higgins, 1981).

Vorauer and Sasaki (2014) identified a number of reasons that imagine-other perspective taking would be more likely than imagine-self perspective taking to lead individuals to consider how an outgroup member might view them in a negative light because of their group membership. In particular, because it centers on understanding another person's point of view, imagine-other perspective taking should be more closely linked to concerns with social evaluation. In addition, because it might be more difficult to imagine another person's unique point of view than what one might think and feel in another person's position, imagine-other perspective taking might be associated with more uncertainty, which can fuel evaluative concerns (Vorauer, 2006). By virtue of an intuitive understanding of ingroup bias, individuals might also be more likely to imagine negative evaluations when trying to appreciate an outgroup member's unique point of view. In line with this theorizing, Vorauer and Sasaki (2014) found that White Canadians who were prompted to engage in imagine-other perspective taking during a written exchange of personal information with an Indigenous Canadian partner evidenced more meta-stereotype activation and less prejudice reduction than did White Canadians who were prompted to engage in imagine-self perspective taking. These findings are broadly consistent with other theoretically based recommendations to promote imagine-self rather than imagine-other perspective taking in tense intergroup conflict situations (e.g., Batson 2009).

Overall, then, to the extent that there is room for a refined focus on the mind-set encouraged and empathy is not contraindicated altogether, prompting imagine-self perspective taking would seem to have the best potential for positive effects in intergroup contexts. For example, in comparison to empathy the implications for targets' power-relevant out-comes are likely to be better.

4.2 Compassion

Compassion is another construct closely related to empathy, one that recently has been the focus of considerable attention. Compassion involves caring about other people's welfare without necessarily feeling their pain (e.g., Bloom, 2017). This definition contrasts especially sharply with the idea of "parallel empathy," which involves experiencing the same emotions that one imagines another to be feeling but is closer to "reactive empathy," which centers on concern for another's well-being and reactions to his or her emotions (Stephan & Finlay, 1999; Todd & Galinsky, 2014). Sometimes referred to as "loving kindness," this mind-set has its roots in Eastern religious traditions. It focuses on intrapsychic processes, with training often involving a meditation component. In connection with this, many of the documented benefits of this mind-set are for the person adopting it, including, for example, enhanced emotional well-being, immune function, and resilience (e.g., Fredrickson et al., 2008; Klimecki et al., 2014; Pace et al., 2009). Research to date on compassion is notable for its neuroscientific approach (e.g., Hutcherson, Seppala, & Gross 2015).

Somewhat similar to the case with social-emotional learning, however, although there is evidence that compassion or loving kindness meditation can foster more positive explicit and implicit evaluations of neutral strangers (Hutcherson, Seppala, & Gross, 2008) and greater helping of a stranger in need (Condon et al., 2013; Weng et al., 2013), the implications of compassion for intergroup attitudes and behavior are less clear. Recalling that enhanced empathy for ingroup members can be associated with more negative attitudes toward outgroup members (Bruneau et al., 2017), it will be important to test whether enhanced prosocial behavior stimulated by compassion extends to treatment of members of disliked groups. Notably, however, Sinclair et al. (2016) found that individuals who were primed with compassionate love – by describing a time when they felt moved to selflessly give of themselves because they wanted the best for another person – reported less prejudiced attitudes toward immigrants than those in various control conditions. These researchers also obtained correlational evidence for a link between chronic levels of compassionate love and behavioral intentions toward immigrants and for more positive implications of compassion than empathy. Because this mind-set incorporates elements of distance and detachment, it would seem perhaps especially promising in the cases involving intractable conflict.

5 Integration with Other Analyses of Empathy

Other analyses of empathic failures and backfiring effects relevant to inter-group relations have recently been advanced. I now consider how the current framework centering on evaluative concerns relates to these analyses and can in some respects provide integration across them.

5.1 Threat

Sassenrath, Hodges, and Pfattheicher (2016) present a model that applies in both interpersonal and intergroup situations for understanding the situations in which perspective taking is likely to backfire. The aforementioned distinctions between perspective taking and empathy notwithstanding, their analysis is highly relevant to understanding the effects of empathy given the considerable overlap between the two constructs. With the core contention that threat to the self is central to backfiring effects, Sassenrath et al. identify three general contexts that involve perceptions of threat. First (context 1), they maintain that threat can arise in connection with characteristics of the target, namely beliefs and values that challenge individuals' self-views in important domains. In essence, the gap is too big and the target is too different, such that moving toward the target through perspective taking would mean losing touch with cherished aspects of self and questioning important values. Second (context 2), they argue that threat can arise when perspective taking leads individuals to imagine how the self might be negatively evaluated by the target. Third (context 3), they argue that perspective taking can be threatening in a negative interdependent context because it leads people to focus on the target's presumed competitive inclinations toward them (see Epley et al., 2006). Notably, the latter two contexts require some form of interaction or exchange, whereas this is not the case for the first – although presumably the implications would be worse there if interaction were involved.

    The second and third contexts identified by Sassenrath et al. overlap quite directly with the present framework in that they center on how perspective taking can lead individuals to focus on targets' potential negative attitudes and behavioral intentions toward them. That is, in both cases perspective taking can be counterproductive by virtue of leading individuals to imagine how a target might be critical of them or be seeking to get the better of them and placing low value on their outcomes. For the first context, namely a "too different" target, Sassenrath et al. argue that the act of perspective taking can lead to a concern about losing important self-aspects that contribute to positive self-evaluation. This element broadens the analysis beyond concerns about evaluation by the target to include concerns about self-evaluation as well.

Sassenrath et al. do not make specific recommendations for intervention. However, the present recommendations to provide additional supports when encouraging empathy in contexts characterized by moderate potential for negative evaluation and to avoid encouraging empathy when there is high potential for negative evaluation would generally seem to apply across all three types of context they identify. Further, although the mapping is surely somewhat imperfect, it may be that the case of a "too different" target (context 1) is also one where the potential for negative evaluation tends to be particularly high. If so, Sassenrath et al.'s analysis suggests an additional reason beyond extreme imagined negative evaluations, namely negative self-evaluations, to avoid encouraging perspective taking in such cases.

5.2 Motivation

Zaki and Cikara (2015) consider a range of different types of empathic failures that may occur and identify three general sources of difficulty that contribute to such failures. They further outline implications for intervention, with a particular emphasis on intergroup contexts. Like the present analysis, their review advocates for a more nuanced approach to understanding empathy and also maintains that additional supports may be needed. In general, these supports involve different means of heightening the motivation for empathy (see also Zaki, 2014), with a focus on using various techniques to motivationally "tune" and prepare individuals to empathize, prior to interaction. These techniques include managing negative emotions prior to encounters through cognitive reappraisal, encouraging malleable lay theories whereby empathy is viewed as a capacity that can be improved (see also Schumann, Zaki, & Dweck, 2014), and highlighting ingroup norms favoring empathic responses (see also Tarrant, Dazeley, & Cottom, 2009).

Many of Zaki and Cikara's (2015) recommendations fit well within the current framework. In particular, viewing empathy as a capacity that can be changed and improved is consistent with the current argument that promoting a learning orientation alongside of empathy may often be beneficial, whether it is focused on learning about outgroup members in particular or a broader orientation toward growth and change.

Further, in many ways encouraging a perception that the ingroup favors empathy should work through mechanisms involving evaluative concern, albeit concern with evaluation by ingroup members rather than outgroup members as emphasized by the present analysis: perceiving an ingroup norm in favor of empathy with an outgroup should motivate individuals to be empathic themselves because of a desire to fit in and be positively regarded by other members of their ingroup. Presumably, such supports would be most effective in intergroup exchanges where the ingroup's perspective is salient, as would be the case if other ingroup members were involved. However, the presence of other ingroup members in intergroup contact situations can increase lower-prejudice individuals' concerns about being viewed in terms of meta-stereotypes by outgroup members (Vorauer, 2003), and these individuals are apt to focus more on how they are viewed by outgroup than ingroup members in intergroup contact situations (Vorauer & Sakamoto, 2008). Further, when prejudice levels are higher or conflict is more intense, there may be resistance and skepticism in response to norm interventions. Thus the dynamics involved in putting these ideas into practice may be complex.

Zaki and Cikara's suggestions regarding managing negative emotions coincide to some extent with the present recommendations to encourage a distanced and analytical mind-set in cases involving extreme hostility. Whether cognitive reappraisal and empathy could be productively implemented in sequence, as per Zaki and Cikara's analysis, or whether distance and detachment are largely incompatible with an empathic orientation – such that it is more a case of "one or the other" – is an intriguing question for future research.

Weisz and Zaki (2017) present a related analysis in which they also consider potential motivational benefits of expanding individuals' perceptions of group boundaries to include outgroup members, as by focusing them on a superordinate identity (see Gaertner et al. 1999). By virtue of being broad and inclusive, superordinate identities can unite individuals from different groups by leading them to see themselves as members of a larger common ingroup rather than as members of distinct groups. For example, White and African Americans might be led to focus on the superordinate identity "Americans." Notably, it is not necessary that original group identities be abandoned. Rather, they can be maintained but within the context of the superordinate identity. Although prompting individuals to think of outgroup members as part of a broader ingroup may both enhance empathy and reduce biases toward them, whether enhanced empathy is a key driving process behind more positive attitudes and behavior or is perhaps more epiphenomenal is unclear. Regardless, to the extent that group boundaries can be successfully broken down, grounds for negativity (including concerns with evaluation) are clearly undermined. Yet serious challenges here include individuals' desire to maintain important specific social identities and feasibility (see Park & Judd, 2005).

The empathy supports suggested in the current analysis, such as enhanced learning orientation and communication, may help with feasibility by facilitating self-other merging and thus may have benefits beyond mitigating evaluative concerns.

6 Summary and Final Considerations

The present analysis highlights a range of complexities and potential difficulties involved in promoting empathy in intergroup contexts and identifies paths to more effective intervention. In considering how individuals' concerns about negative evaluation by outgroup members might lead empathy to backfire, the framework developed here points to alternative mind-sets involving detachment, distance, and reappraisal that are apt to be more beneficial in the context of highly conflictual relations where the perceived potential for negative evaluation is high. It is notable that even – indeed especially – in the case of overtly hostile and aggressive relations where outgroups are dehumanized, individuals' imaginings of outgroup members' judgments of them can fuel negativity. For this reason, it seems that interventions such as empathy that lead individuals' thoughts in the direction of imagining how they are seen by outgroup members should be avoided in these contexts. The present analysis also points to additional supports, such as promoting a learning orientation and enhanced communication, that are apt to set the stage for positive effects of empathy in contexts where the potential for negative evaluation is only moderate, as when groups have limited experience directly interacting. The current framework further identifies contexts, such as those in which individuals are not readily identifiable to outgroup members, in which the beneficial effects of empathy are apt to be most easily achieved and thus where empathy should be readily encouraged.

Concerns with negative evaluation are a function not only of the intergroup context but also the nature of the empathy intervention. Some interventions, such as intergroup dialogue and multicultural education, are very likely to heighten concerns with negative evaluation, whereas others, such as social-emotional learning programs directed at children, are less likely to do so. Other interventions such as direct empathy prompts and intergroup contact are between these two extremes. If one of the approaches that is apt to heighten evaluative concerns is adopted, additional supports may be necessary for positive effects to be realized, and approaches that are most likely to heighten concerns with evaluation seem generally contraindicated in contexts involving high conflict and hostility.

Notably, these recommendations all assume that enhancing warmth- and positivity-relevant intergroup outcomes is a primary consideration. When enhancing power-relevant outcomes of minority group members is a key goal, existing research suggests that encouraging perspective taking rather than empathy is likely to be more beneficial. As well, there are of course other types of important outcomes to consider, such as promoting social structural change, increasing knowledge and awareness, and helping individuals develop an understanding of an outgroup's collective narrative. The recommendations in the present analysis are most applicable to those outcomes for which empathy is helpful, which are unlikely to include all of these. Indeed, the implications of empathy for macro-level intergroup dynamics in particular have been the focus of some debate (e.g., Dixon et al., 2010).

Finally, the present analysis has focused on how considering the influence of evaluative concerns can inform efforts to encourage empathy in intergroup interaction contexts. The evaluative concerns framework provides a means of integrating and organizing diverse research findings, identifying the likely effects of different approaches to intervention, and making theoretically grounded recommendations. Although focusing somewhat narrowly on the evaluative concerns construct helps lend structure and heuristic value to the framework, it is important to acknowledge that a range of other variables are undoubtedly at play in guiding the efficacy of empathy-based interventions. Nonetheless, in view of individuals' very fundamental desire for acceptance and positive regard from others (Leary & Downs, 1995), which does not evaporate in the context of intergroup relations (Vorauer, 2006), considering the influence of these concerns should help identify means of more fully realizing empathy's potential to foster stronger social bonds across group boundaries.

References

Allport, G. W. (1954). *The nature of prejudice*. Cambridge, MA: Addison-Wesley Publishing Company, Inc.

Aron, A., Melinat, E., Aron, E. N., Vallone, R. D., & Bator, R. J. (1997). The experimental generation of interpersonal closeness: A procedure and some preliminary findings. *Personality and Social Psychology Bulletin, 23*, 363–377.

Aronson, E., & Bridgeman, D. (1979). Jigsaw groups and the desegregated classroom: In pursuit of common goals. *Personality and Social Psychology Bulletin, 5*(4), 438–446.

Batson, C. D. (2009). Two forms of perspective taking: Imagining how another feels and imagining how you would feel. In K. D. Markman, W. M. P. Klein, & J. A. Suhr (Eds.), *Handbook of imagination and mental simulation; handbook of imagination and mental simulation* (pp. 267–279). New York: Psychology Press.

Batson, C. D., Ahmad, N., & Lishner, D. A. (2009). Empathy and altruism. In C. D. Batson, N. Ahmad, & D. A. Lishner (Eds.), *Oxford handbook of positive psychology* (2nd ed., pp. 417–426). New York: Oxford University Press.

Batson, C. D., Chang, J., Orr, R., & Rowland, J. (2002). Empathy, attitudes and action: Can feeling for a member of a stigmatized group motivate one to help the group? *Personality and Social Psychology Bulletin, 28*, 1656–1666.

Batson, C. D., Early, S., & Salvarani, G. (1997). Perspective taking: Imagining how another feels versus imagining how you would feel. *Personality and Social Psychology Bulletin, 23*(7), 751–758.

Batson, C. D., Polycarpou, M. P., Harmon-Jones, E., Imhoff, H. J., Mitchener, E. C., Bednar, L. L., ... & Highberger, L. (1997). Empathy and attitudes: Can feeling for a member of a stigmatized group improve feelings toward the group? *Journal of Personality and Social Psychology, 72*, 105–118.

Bergh, R., & Akrami, N. (2016). Are non-agreeable individuals prejudiced? Comparing different conceptualizations of agreeableness. *Personality and Individual Differences, 101*, 153–159.

Bergsieker, H., Shelton, J. N., & Richeson, J. A. (2010). To be liked versus respected: Divergent goals in interracial interactions. *Journal of Personality and Social Psychology, 99*, 248–264.

Berndsen, M., Thomas, E. F., & Pedersen, A. (2018). Resisting perspective-taking: Glorification of the national group elicits noncompliance with perspective-taking instructions. *Journal of Experimental Social Psychology, 79*, 126–137.

Bigler, R. S. (1999). The use of multicultural curricula and materials to counter racism in children. *Journal of Social Issues, 55*(4), 687–705.

Bloom, P. (2017). Empathy and its discontents. *Trends in Cognitive Sciences, 21*(1), 24–31.

Blumberg, H. H. (1972). Communication of interpersonal evaluations. *Journal of Personality and Social Psychology, 23*(2), 157–162.

Bogardus, E. S. (1947). Measurement of personal-group relations. *Sociometry, 10*, 306–311.

Bratt, C. (2008). The jigsaw classroom under test: No effect on intergroup relations evident. *Journal of Community & Applied Social Psychology, 18*(5), 403–419.

Broockman, D., & Kalla, J. (2016). Durably reducing transphobia: A field experiment on door-to-door canvassing. *Science, 352*(6282), 220–224.

Bruneau, E. G., Cikara, M., & Saxe, R. (2017). Parochial empathy predicts reduced altruism and the endorsement of passive harm. *Social Psychological and Personality Science, 8*, 934–942.

Bruneau, E. G., & Saxe, R. (2012). The power of being heard: The benefits of "perspective-giving" in the context of intergroup conflict. *Journal of Experimental Social Psychology, 48*(4), 855–866.

Cameron, L., & Rutland, A. (2006). Extended contact through story-reading in school: Reducing children's prejudice toward the disabled. *Journal of Social Issues, 62*, 469–488.

Case, K. A. (2007). Raising white privilege awareness and reducing racial prejudice: Assessing diversity course effectiveness. *Teaching of Psychology, 34*(4), 231–235.

Cehajic, S., Brown, R., & Castano, E. (2008). Forgive and forget? Antecedents and consequences of intergroup forgiveness in Bosnia and Herzegovina. *Political Psychology, 29*(3), 351–367.

Cikara, M., Bruneau, E. G., & Saxe, R. R. (2011). Us and them: Intergroup failures of empathy. *Current Directions in Psychological Science, 20*, 149–153.

Clore, G. L., & Jeffery, K. M. (1972). Emotional role playing, attitude change, and attraction toward a disabled person. *Journal of Personality and Social Psychology, 23*(1), 105–111.

Coke, J. S., Batson, C. D., & McDavis, K. (1978). Empathic mediation of helping: A two-stage model. *Journal of Personality and Social Psychology, 36*, 752–766.

Collaborative for Academic, Social, and Emotional Learning. (2003). *Safe and sound: An educational leader's guide to evidence based social and emotional learning (SEL) programs*. Chicago: Author.

Condon, P., Desbordes, G., Miller, W. B., & DeSteno, D. (2013). Meditation increases compassionate responses to suffering. *Psychological Science, 24*(10), 2125–2127.

Correll, J., Park, B., & Smith, J. A. (2008). Colorblind and multicultural prejudice reduction strategies in high-conflict situations. *Group Processes & Intergroup Relations, 11*(4), 471–491.

Cortland, C. I., Craig, M. A., Shapiro, J. R., Richeson, J. A., Neel, R., & Goldstein, N. J. (2017). Solidarity through shared disadvantage: Highlighting shared experiences of discrimination improves relations between stigmatized groups. *Journal of Personality and Social Psychology, 113*(4), 547–567.

Cuff, B. M. P., Brown, S. J., Taylor, L., & Howat, D. J. (2016). Empathy: A review of the concept. *Emotion Review, 8*(2), 144–153.

Darley, J. M & Gross, P. H. (1983). A hypothesis-confirming bias in labeling effects. *Journal of Personality and Social Psychology, 44*, 20–33.

Davies, K., Tropp, L. R., Aron, A., Pettigrew, T. F., & Wright, S. C. (2011). Cross-group friendships and intergroup attitudes: A meta-analytic review. *Personality and Social Psychology Review, 15*(4), 332–351.

Davis, M. H. (1983). The effects of dispositional empathy on emotional reactions and helping: A multidimensional approach. *Journal of Personality, 51*, 167–184.

Davis, M. H., Conklin, L., Smith, A., & Luce, C. (1996). Effect of perspective-taking on the cognitive representation of persons: A merging of self and other. *Journal of Personality and Social Psychology, 70*, 713–726.

Devine, P. G., Evett, S. R., & Vasquez-Suson, K. A. (1996). Exploring the interpersonal dynamics of intergroup contact. In R. Sorrentino & E. T. Higgins (Eds.), *Handbook of motivation and cognition: The interpersonal context* (Vol. 3, pp. 423–464). New York: Guildford Press.

Ditlmann, R. K., & Samii, C. (2016). Can intergroup contact affect ingroup dynamics? Insights from a field study with Jewish and Arab-Palestinian youth in Israel. *Peace and Conflict: Journal of Peace Psychology, 22*(4), 380–392.

Dixon, J., Levine, M., Reicher, S., & Durrheim, K. (2012). Beyond prejudice: Are negative evaluations the problem and is getting us to like one another more the solution? *Behavioral and Brain Sciences, 35*, 411–425.

Dixon, J., Tropp, L. R., Durrheim, K., & Tredoux, C. (2010). "Let them eat harmony": Prejudice-reduction strategies and attitudes of historically disadvantaged groups. *Current Directions in Psychological Science, 19*(2), 76–80.

Dovidio, J. F., ten Vergert, M., Stewart, T. L., Gaertner, S. L., Johnson, J. D., Esses, V. M. ... & Pearson, A. R. (2004). Perspective and prejudice: Antecedents and mediating mechanisms. *Personality and Social Psychology Bulletin, 30*, 1537–1549.

Dunn, E. W., Biesanz, J. C., Human, L. J., & Finn, S. (2007). Misunderstanding the affective consequences of everyday social interactions: The hidden benefits of putting one's best face forward. *Journal of Personality and Social Psychology, 92*, 990–1005.

Dutra, N. B., Boccardi, N. C., Silva, P. R. R., Siqueira, J. d. O., Hattori, W. T., Yamamoto, M. E., & de Alencar, A. I. (2018). Adult criticism and vigilance diminish free riding by children in a social dilemma. *Journal of Experimental Child Psychology, 167*, 1–9.

Elliott, J. (2017). It's all about ignorance: Reflections from the blue-eyed/brown-eyed exercise. In C. G. Sibley & F. K. Barlow (Eds.), *The Cambridge handbook of the psychology of prejudice* (pp. 655–668). New York: Cambridge University Press.

Epley, N., Caruso, E., & Bazerman, M. H. (2006). When perspective taking increases taking: Reactive egoism in social interaction. *Journal of Personality and Social Psychology, 91*, 872–889.

Eyal, T., Steffel, M., & Epley, N. (2018). Perspective mistaking: Accurately understanding the mind of another requires getting perspective, not taking perspective. *Journal of Personality and Social Psychology, 114*(4), 547–571.

Farmer, H., & Maister, L. (2017). Putting ourselves in another's skin: Using the plasticity of self-perception to enhance empathy and decrease prejudice. *Social Justice Research, 30*, 323–354.

Finkel, E. J., Slotter, E. B., Luchies, L. B., Walton, G. M., & Gross, J. J. (2013). A brief intervention to promote conflict reappraisal preserves marital quality over time. *Psychological Science, 24*, 1595–1601.

Finlay, K. A., & Stephan, W. G. (2000). Improving intergroup relations: The effects of empathy on racial attitudes. *Journal of Applied Social Psychology, 30*, 1720–1737.

Fredrickson, B. L., Cohn, M. A., Coffey, K. A., Pek, J., & Finkel, S. M. (2008). Open hearts build lives: Positive emotions, induced through loving-kindness meditation, build consequential personal resources. *Journal of Personality and Social Psychology, 95*(5), 1045–1062.

Gaertner, S. L., Dovidio, J. F., Nier, J. A., Ward, C. M., & Banker, B. S. (1999). Across cultural divides: The value of a superordinate identity. In D. Prentice

& D. Miller (Eds.), *Cultural divides: Understanding and overcoming group conflict* (pp. 173–212). New York: Sage.

Galinsky, A. D., Ku, G., & Wang, C. S. (2005). Perspective-taking and self-other overlap: Fostering social bonds and facilitating social coordination. *Group Processes & Intergroup Relations, 8*(2), 109–124.

Galinsky, A. D., Maddux, W. W., Glin, D., & White, J. B. (2008). Why it pays to get inside the head of your opponent: The differential effects of perspective taking and empathy in negotiations. *Psychological Science, 19*, 378–384.

Galinsky, A. D., Magee, J. C., Inesi, M. E., & Gruenfeld, D. H. (2006). Power and perspectives not taken. *Psychological Science, 17*, 1068–1074.

Galinsky, A. D., & Moskowitz, G. B. (2000). Perspective-taking: Decreasing stereotype expression, stereotype accessibility, and in-group favoritism. *Journal of Personality and Social Psychology,78*, 708–724.

Galinsky, A. D., Wang, C. S., & Ku, G. (2008). Perspective-takers behave more stereotypically. *Journal of Personality and Social Psychology, 95*, 404–419.

Garriott, P. O., Reiter, S., & Brownfield, J. (2016). Testing the efficacy of brief multicultural education interventions in white college students. *Journal of Diversity in Higher Education, 9*(2), 158–169.

Gilin, D., Maddux, W. W., Carpenter, J., & Galinsky, A. D. (2013). When to use your head and when to use your heart: The differential value of perspective-taking versus empathy in competitive interactions. *Personality and Social Psychology Bulletin, 39*(1), 3–16.

Goldenberg, A., Endevelt, K., Ran, S., Dweck, C. S, Gross, J. J., & Halperin, E. (2017). Making intergroup contact more fruitful: Enhancing cooperation between Palestinian and Jewish-Israeli adolescents by fostering beliefs about group malleability. *Social Psychological and Personality Science, 8*, 3–10.

Goldstein, N. J., Vezich, I. S., & Shapiro, J. R. (2014). Perceived perspective taking: When others walk in our shoes. *Journal of Personality and Social Psychology, 106*(6), 941–960.

Greenland, K., Xenias, D., & Maio, G. R. (2017). Effects of promotion and compunction interventions on real intergroup interactions: Promotion helps but high compunction hurts. *Frontiers in Psychology, 8*, 10.

Greenwald, A. G., McGhee, D. E., & Schwartz, J. L. K. (1998). Measuring individual differences in implicit cognition: The Implicit Association Test. *Journal of Personality and Social Psychology, 74*, 1464–1480.

Groom, V., Bailenson, J. N., & Nass, C. (2009). The influence of racial embodiment on racial bias in immersive virtual environments. *Social Influence, 4*(3), 231–248.

Grossmann, I., & Kross, E. (2014). Exploring Solomon's paradox: Self-distancing eliminates the self-other asymmetry in wise reasoning about close relationships in younger and older adults. *Psychological Science*, *25*(8), 1571–1580.

Guffler, K., & Wagner, U. (2017). Backfire of good intentions: Unexpected long-term contact intervention effects in an intractable conflict area. *Peace and Conflict: Journal of Peace Psychology*, *23*(4), 383–391.

Gutsell, J. N., & Inzlicht, M. (2012). Intergroup differences in the sharing of emotive states: Neural evidence of an empathy gap. *Social Cognitive and Affective Neuroscience*, *7*(5), 596–603.

Halabi, S., Dovidio, J. F., & Nadler, A. (2016). Help that hurts? Perceptions of intergroup assistance. *International Journal of Intercultural Relations*, *53*, 65–71.

Halabi, S., & Nadler, A. (2017). The intergroup status as helping relations model: Giving, seeking and receiving help as tools to maintain or challenge social inequality. In E. van Leeuwen & H. Zagefka (Eds.), *Intergroup helping* (pp. 205–221). Cham, Switzerland: Springer International Publishing AG.

Halperin, E., Porat, R., Tamir, M., & Gross, J. J. (2013). Can emotion regulation change political attitudes in intractable conflicts? From the laboratory to the field. corrigendum. *Psychological Science*, *25*(11), 2120.

Hasson, Y., Tamir, M., Brahms, K. S., Cohrs, J. C., & Halperin, E. (2018). Are liberals and conservatives equally motivated to feel empathy toward others? *Personality and Social Psychology Bulletin*, *44*, 1449–1459.

Higgins, E. T. (1981). Role taking and social judgment: Alternative developmental perspectives and processes. In J. H. Flavell & L. Ross (Eds.), *Social cognitive development: Frontiers and possible futures* (pp. 119–153). New York: Cambridge University Press.

Hodges, S. D., Clark, B. A. M., & Myers, M. W. (2011). *Better living through perspective taking* (pp. 193–218). New York: Springer Science + Business Media.

Holoien, D. S., Libby, L. K., & Shelton, J. N. (2016, January). *Racial minorities' reactions to Whites' expressions of empathy and sympathy*. Presented at the annual meeting of the Social for Personality and Social Psychology, San Diego, CA.

Hornsey, M. J., & Esposo, S. (2009). Resistance to group criticism and recommendations for change: Lessons from the intergroup sensitivity effect. *Social and Personality Psychology Compass*, *3*(3), 275–291.

Hornsey, M. J., & Wohl, M. J. A. (2013) We are sorry: Intergroup apologies and their tenuous link with intergroup forgiveness, *European Review of Social Psychology*, *24*(*1*), 1–31. doi:10.1080/10463283.2013.822206

Huang, K., Yeomans, M., Brooks, A. W., Minson, J., & Gino, F. (2017). It doesn't hurt to ask: Question-asking increases liking. *Journal of Personality and Social Psychology, 113*(3), 430–452.

Hutcherson, C. A., Seppala, E. M., & Gross, J. J. (2008). Loving-kindness meditation increases social connectedness. *Emotion, 8*(5), 720–724.

Hutcherson, C. A., Seppala, E. M., & Gross, J. J. (2015). The neural correlates of social connection. *Cognitive, Affective & Behavioral Neuroscience, 15*(1), 1–14.

Idan, O., Halperin, E., Hameiri, B., & Tagar, M. R. (2018). A rose by any other name? A subtle linguistic cue impacts anger and corresponding policy support in intractable conflict. *Psychological Science, 29*, 972–983.

Kenny, D. A., & DePaulo, B. M. (1993). Do people know how others view them? An empirical and theoretical account. *Psychological Bulletin, 114*, 145–161.

Kernahan, C., & Davis, T. (2010). What are the long-term effects of learning about racism? *Teaching of Psychology, 37*(1), 41–45.

Klimecki, O. M., Leiberg, S., Ricard, M., & Singer, T. (2014). Differential pattern of functional brain plasticity after compassion and empathy training. *Social Cognitive and Affective Neuroscience, 9*(6), 873–879.

Kross, E., & Ayduk, O. (2008). Facilitating adaptive emotional analysis: Distinguishing distanced-analysis of depressive experiences from immersed-analysis and distraction. *Personality and Social Psychology Bulletin, 34*(7), 924–938.

Kross, E., Ayduk, O., & Mischel, W. (2005). When asking "why" does not hurt: Distinguishing rumination from reflective processing of negative emotions. *Psychological Science, 16*(9), 709–715.

Krueger, J. (1996). Personal beliefs and cultural stereotypes about racial characteristics. *Journal of Personality and Social Psychology, 71*(3), 536–548.

Kteily, N., Hodson, G., & Bruneau, E. (2016). They see us as less than human: Metadehumanization predicts intergroup conflict via reciprocal dehumanization. *Journal of Personality and Social Psychology, 110*(3), 343–370.

Lai, C. K., Marini, M., Lehr, S. A., Cerruti, C., Shin, J. L., Joy-Gaba, J., . . . & Nosek, B. A. (2014). Reducing implicit racial preferences: I. A comparative investigation of 17 interventions. *Journal of Experimental Psychology: General, 143*(4), 1765–1785.

Lazarus, N. (2015). Evaluating seeds of peace: Assessing long-term impact in volatile context. In C. Del Felice, A. Karako, & A. Wisler (Eds.), *Peace education evaluation: Learning from experience and exploring prospects;*

peace education evaluation: Learning from experience and exploring pro-spects (pp. 163–177). Charlotte, NC: IAP Information Age Publishing.

Leary, M. R., & Downs, D. L. (1995). Interpersonal functions of the self-esteem motive: The self-esteem system as sociometer. In M. H. Kernis (Ed.), *Efficacy, agency, and self-esteem* (pp. 123–144). New York: Plenum Press.

Leary, M. R., Kowalski, R. M., & Bergen, D. J. (1988). Interpersonal informa-tion acquisition and confidence in first encounters. *Personality and Social Psychology Bulletin, 14*(1), 68–77.

Levy, S. R., & Dweck, C. S. (1999). The impact of children's static versus dynamic conceptions of people on stereotype formation. *Child Development, 70*(5), 1163–1180.

Levy, S. R., Stroessner, S. J., & Dweck, C. S. (1998). Stereotype formation and endorsement: The role of implicit theories. *Journal of Personality and Social Psychology, 74*, 1421–1436.

MacInnis, C. C., & Page-Gould, E. (2015). How can intergroup interaction be bad if intergroup contact is good? Exploring and reconciling an apparent paradox in the science of intergroup relations. *Perspectives on Psychological Science, 10*(3), 307–327.

Madera, J. M., Neal, J. A., & Dawson, M. (2011). A strategy for diversity training: Focusing on empathy in the workplace. *Journal of Hospitality & Tourism Research, 35*(4), 469–487.

Maister, L., Slater, M., Sanchez-Vives, M., & Tsakiris, M. (2015). Changing bodies changes minds: Owning another body affects social cognition. *Trends in Cognitive Sciences, 19*(1), 6–12.

Ma-Kellams, C., & Lerner, J. (2016). Trust your gut or think carefully? Examining whether an intuitive, versus a systematic, mode of thought produces greater empathic accuracy. *Journal of Personality and Social Psychology, 111*, 674–685.

Malhotra, D., & Liyanage, S. (2005). Long-term effects of peace workshops in protracted conflicts. *The Journal of Conflict Resolution, 49*(6), 908–924.

Mallett, R. M., Wilson, T. D., & Gilbert, D. T. (2008). Expect the unexpected: Failure to anticipate similarities leads to an intergroup forecasting error. *Journal of Personality and Social Psychology, 94*, 265–277.

Malti, T., Chaparro, M. P., Zuffianò, A., & Colasante, T. (2016). School-based interventions to promote empathy-related responding in children and adolescents: A developmental analysis. *Journal of Clinical Child and Adolescent Psychology, 45*(6), 718–731.

Martin, P. (2018, May). Bridging the gap between Arabs and Jews, in Ontario Lake country. Retrieved from www.theglobeandmail.com/news/world/camp-shomria-bridging-the-gap-between-arabs-and-jews-in-ontario-lake-country/article13587005/

McConahay, J. G., Hardee, B. B., & Batts, V. (1981). Has racism declined? It depends on who's asking and what is asked. *Journal of Conflict Resolution, 25*, 563–579.

McFarland, S. (2010). Authoritarianism, social dominance, and other roots of generalized prejudice. *Political Psychology, 31*(3), 453–477.

Miklikowska, M. (2018). Empathy trumps prejudice: The longitudinal relation between empathy and anti-immigrant attitudes in adolescence. *Developmental Psychology, 54*(4), 703–717.

Mooijman, M., & Stern, C. (2016). When perspective taking creates a motivational threat: The case of conservatism, same-sex sexual behavior, and anti-gay attitudes. *Personality and Social Psychology Bulletin, 42*(6), 738–754.

Murphy, M. C., Richeson, J. A., & Molden, D. C. (2011). Leveraging motivational mindsets to foster positive interracial interactions. *Social and Personality Psychology Compass, 5*(2), 118–131.

Nadler, A., & Liviatan, I. (2006). Intergroup reconciliation: Effects of adversary's expressions of empathy, responsibility, and recipients' trust. *Personality and Social Psychology Bulletin, 32*(4), 459–470.

Nadler, A., & Shnabel, N. (2015). Intergroup reconciliation: Instrumental and socio-emotional processes and the needs-based model. *European Review of Social Psychology, 26*(1), 93–125.

Oh, S. Y., Bailenson, J., Weisz, E., & Zaki, J. (2016). Virtually old: Embodied perspective taking and the reduction of ageism under threat. *Computers in Human Behavior, 60*, 398–410.

Okimoto, T. G., & Wenzel, M. (2011). The other side of perspective taking: Transgression ambiguity and victims' revenge against their offender. *Social Psychological and Personality Science, 2*, 373–378.

Pace, T. W. W., Negi, L. T., Adame, D. D., Cole, S. P., Sivilli, T. I., Brown, T. D., . . . & Raison, C. L. (2009). Effect of compassion meditation on neuroendocrine, innate immune and behavioral responses to psychosocial stress. *Psychoneuroendocrinology, 34*(1), 87–98.

Page-Gould, E., Mendoza-Denton, R., & Tropp, L. R. (2008). With a little help from my cross-group friend: Reducing anxiety in intergroup contexts through cross-group friendship. *Journal of Personality and Social Psychology, 95*, 1080–1094.

Paluck, E. L. (2009). Reducing intergroup prejudice and conflict using the media: A field experiment in Rwanda. *Journal of Personality and Social Psychology, 96*, 574–587.

Paluck, E. L. (2010). Is it better not to talk? Group polarization, extended contact, and perspective taking in eastern Democratic Republic of Congo. *Personality and Social Psychology Bulletin, 36*, 1170–1185.

Paluck, E. L. (2016. How to overcome prejudice: A brief conversation can have a lasting effect on prejudice. *Science, 352*, 147.

Paluck, E. L., & Green, D. P. (2009). Prejudice reduction: What works? A review and assessment of research and practice. *Annual Review of Psychology, 60*, 339–367.

Paluck, E. L., Green, S. A., & Green, D. P. (2018). The contact hypothesis re-evaluated. *Behavioral Public Policy*, 1–30. Cambridge University Press. doi:10.1017/bpp.2018.25

Paolini, S., Harwood, J., & Rubin, M. (2010). Negative intergroup contact makes group memberships salient: Explaining why intergroup conflict endures. *Personality and Social Psychology Bulletin, 36*(12), 1723–1738.

Paolini, S., Hewstone, M., Cairns, E., & Voci, A. (2004). Effects of direct and indirect cross-group friendships on judgments of Catholics and Protestants in Northern Ireland: The mediating role of an anxiety-reduction mechanism. *Personality and Social Psychology Bulletin, 30*, 770–786.

Park, B. J., & Judd, C. M. (2005). Rethinking the link between categorization and prejudice within the social cognition perspective. *Personality and Social Psychology Review, 9*, 108–130.

Pearce, K., & Ross, S. (Producers). (1991, September 26). *Primetime live* [Television broadcast]. New York: ABC News.

Pecukonis, E. (1990). A cognitive/affective empathy training program. *Adolescence, 25*(97), 59.

Peters, W. (Producer/Director). (1971). *The eye of the storm* [Television movie]. New York: American Broadcasting Company.

Pettigrew, T. F. (1998). Intergroup contact theory. *Annual Review of Psychology, 49*, 65–85.

Pettigrew, T. F., & Tropp, L. R. (2006). A meta-analytic test of intergroup contact theory. *Journal of Personality and Social Psychology, 90*, 751–783.

Pettigrew, T. F., & Tropp, L. R. (2008). How does intergroup contact reduce prejudice? Meta-analytic tests of three mediators. *European Journal of Social Psychology, 38*(6), 922–934.

Pierce, J. R., Kilduff, G. J., Galinsky, A. D., & Sivanathan, N. (2013). From glue to gasoline: How competition turns perspective takers unethical. *Psychological Science, 24*(10), 1986–1994.

Pliskin, R., Bar-Tal, D., Sheppes, G., & Halperin, E. (2014). Are leftists more emotion-driven than rightists? The interactive influence of ideology and emotions on support for policies. *Personality & Social Psychology Bulletin, 40*(12), 1681–1697.

Porat, R., Halperin, E., & Tamir, M. (2016). What we want is what we get: Group-based emotional preferences and conflict resolution. *Journal of Personality and Social Psychology, 110*, 167–190.

Quintana, S. M. (1994). A model of ethnic perspective-taking ability applied to Mexican-American children and youth. *International Journal of Intercultural Relations, 18*(4), 419–448.

Quintana, S. M. (1998). Children's developmental understanding of ethnicity and race. *Applied & Preventive Psychology, 7*(1), 27–45.

Richeson, J. A., & Shelton, J. N. (2003). When prejudice does not pay: Effects of interracial contact on executive function. *Psychological Science, 14*, 287–90.

Richeson, J. A., & Trawalter, S. (2005). Why do interracial interactions impair executive function? A resource depletion account. *Journal of Personality and Social Psychology, 88*(6), 934–947.

Roseth, C. J., Johnson, D. W., & Johnson, R. T. (2008). Promoting early adolescents' achievement and peer relationships: The effects of cooperative, competitive, and individualistic goal structures. *Psychological Bulletin, 134*(2), 223–246.

Rosler, N., Cohen-Chen, S., & Halperin, E. (2017). The distinctive effects of empathy and hope in intractable conflicts. *Journal of Conflict Resolution, 61*, 114–139.

Salomon, G. (2004). A narrative-based view of coexistence education. *Journal of Social Issues, 60*(2), 273–287.

Sasaki, S. J., & Vorauer, J. D. (2010). Contagious resource depletion and anxiety? Spreading effects of evaluative concern and impression formation in dyadic social interaction. *Journal of Experimental Social Psychology, 46*, 1011–1016.

Sassenrath, C., Hodges, S. D., & Pfattheicher, S. (2016). It's all about the self: When perspective taking backfires. *Current Directions in Psychological Science, 25*(6), 405–410.

Schneider, M. E., Major, B., Luhtanen, R., & Crocker, J. (1996). Social stigma and the potential costs of assumptive help. *Personality and Social Psychology Bulletin, 22*(2), 201–209.

Schonert-Reichl, K., Smith, V., Zaidman-Zait, A., & Hertzman, C. (2012). Promoting children's prosocial behaviors in school: Impact of the "roots of empathy" program on the social and emotional competence of school-aged children. *School Mental Health, 4*(1), 1–21.

Schumann, K., Zaki, J., & Dweck, C. S. (2014). Addressing the empathy deficit: Beliefs about the malleability of empathy predict effortful responses when empathy is challenging. *Journal of Personality and Social Psychology, 107*(3), 475–493.

Shaw, A., Montinari, N., Piovesan, M., Olson, K. R., Gino, F., & Norton, M. I. (2014). Children develop a veil of fairness. *Journal of Experimental Psychology: General, 143*(1), 363–375.

Shechtman, Z., & Tanus, H. (2006). Counseling groups for Arab adolescents in an intergroup conflict in Israel: Report of an outcome study. *Peace and Conflict: Journal of Peace Psychology, 12*(2), 119–137.

Shelton, J. N., & Richeson, J. A. (2005). Intergroup contact and pluralistic ignorance. *Journal of Personality and Social Psychology, 88*, 91–107.

Shih, M. J., Stotzer, R., & Gutiérrez, A. S. (2013). Perspective-taking and empathy: Generalizing the reduction of group bias towards Asian Americans to general outgroups. *Asian American Journal of Psychology, 4*(2), 79–83.

Sierksma, J., Thijs, J., & Verkuyten, M. (2015). In-group bias in children's intention to help can be overpowered by inducing empathy. *British Journal of Developmental Psychology, 33*(1), 45–56. doi:10.1111/bjdp.12065

Silverman, A. M., Gwinn, J. D., & Van Boven, L. (2015). Stumbling in their shoes: Disability simulations reduce judged capabilities of disabled people. *Social Psychological and Personality Science, 6*(4), 464–471.

Sinclair, L., Fehr, B., Wang, W., & Regehr, E. (2016). The relation between compassionate love and prejudice: The mediating role of inclusion of out-group members in the self. *Social Psychological and Personality Science, 7*(2), 176–183.

Sleeter, C., & Grant, C. (1987) An analysis of multicultural education in the United States. *Harvard Educational Review: December, 57*(4), 421–445.

Soble, J. R., Spanierman, L. B., & Liao, H. (2011). Effects of a brief video intervention on white university students' racial attitudes. *Journal of Counseling Psychology, 58*(1), 151–157.

Spanierman, L. B., & Heppner, M. J. (2004). Psychosocial Costs of Racism to Whites Scale (PCRW): Construction and initial validation. *Journal of Counseling Psychology, 51*(2), 249–262.

Stephan, W. G., & Finlay, K. (1999). The role of empathy in improving intergroup relations. *Journal of Social Issues, 55*(4), 729–743.

Stewart, T. L., LaDuke, J. R., Bracht, C., Sweet, B. A. M., & Gamarel, K. E. (2003). Do the "eyes" have it? A program evaluation of Jane Elliott's "blue-eyes/brown-eyes" diversity training exercise. *Journal of Applied Social Psychology, 33*(9), 1898–1921.

Tarrant, M., Calitri, R., & Weston, D. (2012). Social identification structures the effects of perspective taking. *Psychological Science, 23*, 973–978.

Tarrant, M., Dazeley, S., & Cottom, T. (2009). Social categorization and empathy for outgroup members. *British Journal of Social Psychology, 48*(3), 427–446.

Thompson, L. L. (1991). Information exchange in negotiation. *Journal of Experimental Social Psychology, 27*(2), 161–179.

Thürmer, J. L., & McCrea, S. M. (in press). Beyond motivated reasoning: Hostile reactions to critical comments from the outgroup. *Motivation Science.*

Todd, A. R., Bodenhausen, G. V., Richeson, J. A., & Galinsky, A. D. (2011). Perspective taking combats automatic expressions of racial bias. *Journal of Personality and Social Psychology, 100*, 1027–1042.

Todd, A. R., & Galinsky, A. D. (2012). The reciprocal link between multiculturalism and perspective taking: How ideological and self-regulatory approaches to managing diversity reinforce each other? *Journal of Experimental Social Psychology, 48*(6), 1394–1398.

Todd, A. R., & Galinsky, A. D. (2014). Perspective-taking as a strategy for improving intergroup relations: Evidence, mechanisms, and qualifications. *Social and Personality Psychology Compass, 8*(7), 374–387.

Todd, A. R., Galinsky, A. D., & Bodenhausen, G. V. (2012). Perspective taking undermines stereotype maintenance processes: Evidence from social memory, behavior explanation, and information solicitation. *Social Cognition, 30*, 94–108.

Trawalter, S., & Richeson, J. A. (2006). Regulatory focus and executive function after interracial interactions. *Journal of Experimental Social Psychology, 42*(3), 406–412.

Tropp, L. R., & Barlow, F. K. (2018). Making advantaged racial groups care about inequality: Intergroup contact as a route to psychological investment. *Current Directions in Psychological Science, 27*(3). doi.org/10.1177/0963721417743282

Trost, M. R., Cialdini, R. B., & Maass, A. (1989). Effects of an international conflict simulation on perceptions of the Soviet Union: A FIREBREAKS backfire. *Journal of Social Issues, 45*(2), 139–158.

van Berkhout, E., & Malouff, J. (2016). The efficacy of empathy training: A meta-analysis of randomized controlled trials. *Journal of Counseling Psychology, 63,* 32–41.

Vescio, T. K., Sechrist, G. B., & Paolucci, M. P. (2003). Perspective taking and prejudice reduction: The mediational role of empathy arousal and situational attributions. *European Journal of Social Psychology, 33*, 455–472.

Vorauer, J. D. (2003). Dominant group members in intergroup interaction: Safety or vulnerability in numbers? *Personality and Social Psychology Bulletin, 29*, 498–511.

Vorauer, J. D. (2005). Miscommunications surrounding efforts to reach out across group boundaries. *Personality and Social Psychology Bulletin, 31*, 1653–1664.

Vorauer, J. D. (2006). An information search model of evaluative concerns in intergroup interaction. *Psychological Review, 113*, 862–886.

Vorauer, J. D. (2008). Unprejudiced and self-focused: When intergroup contact is experienced as being about the ingroup rather than the outgroup. *Journal of Experimental Social Psychology, 44*, 912–919.

Vorauer, J. D. (2012). Completing the Implicit Association Test (IAT) reduces positive intergroup interaction behavior. *Psychological Science, 23*, 1168–1175.

Vorauer, J. D. (2013). The case for and against perspective-taking. In M. P. Zanna & J. Olson (Eds.), *Advances in experimental social psychology*, vol. 48, pp. 59–115. Burlington: Academic Press.

Vorauer, J. D. (2018). *Perceived and self-reported empathy in intergroup interaction*. Unpublished raw data.

Vorauer, J. D., & Cameron, J. J. (2002). So close, and yet so far: Does collectivism foster transparency overestimation? *Journal of Personality and Social Psychology, 83*, 1344–1352.

Vorauer, J. D., Gagnon, A., & Sasaki, S. J. (2009). Salient intergroup ideology and intergroup interaction. *Psychological Science, 20*, 838–845.

Vorauer, J. D., Main, K. J., & O'Connell, G. B. (1998). How do individuals expect to be viewed by members of lower status groups? Content and implications of meta-stereotypes. *Journal of Personality and Social Psychology, 75*, 917–937.

Vorauer, J. D., & Martens, V., & Sasaki, S. J. (2009). When trying to understand detracts from trying to behave: Effects of perspective-taking in intergroup interaction. *Journal of Personality and Social Psychology, 96*, 811–827.

Vorauer, J. D., & Petsnik, C. (2018). *What really helps? Divergent implications of talking to someone with an empathic mind-set versus similar experience for shame and self-evaluation in the wake of an embarrassing event*. Manuscript under review.

Vorauer, J. D., & Quesnel, M. (2016). Don't bring me down: Divergent effects of being the target of empathy versus perspective-taking on minority group members' perceptions of their group's social standing. *Group Processes and Intergroup Relations, 19*, 94–109.

Vorauer, J. D., & Quesnel, M. (2017a). Ideology and voice: Salient multi-culturalism enhances minority group members' persuasiveness in intergroup interaction. *Social Psychological and Personality Science, 8*(8), 867–874.

Vorauer, J. D., & Quesnel, M. (2017b). Salient multiculturalism enhances minority group members' feelings of power. *Personality and Social Psychology Bulletin, 43*, 259–271.

Vorauer, J. D., & Quesnel, M. (2018). Empathy by dominant versus minority group members in intergroup interaction: Do dominant group members always come out on top? *Group Processes and Intergroup Relations, 21*, 549–567.

Vorauer, J. D., Quesnel, M., & Germain, S. L. (2016). Reductions in goal-directed cognition as a consequence of being the target of empathy. *Personality and Social Psychology Bulletin, 42*, 130–141.

Vorauer, J. D., & Sakamoto, Y. (2006). I thought we could be friends, but … Systematic miscommunication and defensive distancing as obstacles to cross-group friendship formation. *Psychological Science, 17*, 326–331.

Vorauer, J. D., & Sakamoto, Y. (2008). Who cares what the outgroup thinks? Testing an information search model of the importance individuals accord to an outgroup member's view of them during intergroup interaction. *Journal of Personality and Social Psychology, 95*, 1467–1480.

Vorauer, J. D., & Sasaki, S. J. (2009). Helpful only in the abstract? Ironic effects of empathy in intergroup interaction. *Psychological Science, 20*, 191–197.

Vorauer, J. D., & Sasaki, S. J. (2011). In the worst rather than the best of times: Effects of salient intergroup ideology in threatening intergroup interactions. *Journal of Personality and Social Psychology, 101*, 307–320.

Vorauer, J. D., & Sasaki, S. J. (2014). Distinct effects of imagine-other versus imagine-self perspective-taking on prejudice reduction. *Social Cognition, 32*, 130–147.

Vorauer, J. D., & Sucharyna, T. (2013). Potential negative effects of perspective-taking efforts in the context of close relationships: Increased bias and reduced satisfaction. *Journal of Personality and Social Psychology, 104*, 70–86.

Vorauer, J. D., & Turpie, C. (2004). Relation of prejudice to choking versus shining under pressure in intergroup interaction: The disruptive effects of vigilance. *Journal of Personality and Social Psychology, 87*, 384–399.

Weisz, E., & Zaki, J. (2017). Empathy-building interventions: A review of existing work and suggestions for future directions. In E. M. Seppälä, E. Simon-Thomas, S. L. Brown, M. C. Worline, C. D. Cameron & J. R. Doty (Eds.), *The Oxford handbook of compassion science* (pp. 205–217). New York: Oxford University Press.

Weng, H. Y., Fox, A. S., Shackman, A. J., Stodola, D. E., Caldwell, J. Z. K., Olson, M. C., ... & Davidson, R. J. (2013). Compassion training alters altruism and neural responses to suffering. *Psychological Science*, *24*(7), 1171–1180.

West, K., & Greenland, K. (2016). Beware of "reducing prejudice": Imagined contact may backfire if applied with a prevention focus. *Journal of Applied Social Psychology*, *46*(10), 583–592.

Wilkes, M., Milgrom, E., & Hoffman, J. R. (2002). Towards more empathic medical students: A medical student hospitalization experience. *Medical Education*, *36*(6), 528–533.

Wilson, T. D., Dunn, D. S., Kraft, D. & Lisle, D. J. (1989). Introspection, attitude change, and attitude-behavior consistency: The disruptive effects of explaining why we feel the way we do. In L. Berkowitz (Ed.), *Advances in experimental social psychology*, Vol. 22, pp. 287–343). New York: Academic Press.

Winczewski, L. A., Bowen, J. D., & Collins, N. L. (2016). Is empathic accuracy enough to facilitate responsive behavior in dyadic interaction? Distinguishing ability from motivation. *Psychological Science*, *27*(3), 394–404.

Wright, S. C., Aron, A., McLaughlin-Volpe, T., & Ropp, S. A. (1997). The extended contact effect: Knowledge of cross-group friendships and prejudice. *Journal of Personality and Social Psychology*, *73*, 73–90.

Wright, S. C., Mazziotta, A., & Tropp, L. R. (2017). Contact and intergroup conflict: New ideas for the road ahead. *Peace and Conflict: Journal of Peace Psychology*, *23*(3), 317–327.

Zaki, J. (2014). Empathy: A motivated account. *Psychological Bulletin*, *140*(6), 1608–1647.

Zaki, J., & Cikara, M. (2015). Addressing empathic failures. *Current Directions in Psychological Science*, *24*(6), 471–476.

Zuckerman, M., Kernis, M. H., Guarnera, S. M., Murphy, J. F., & Rappoport, L. (1983). The egocentric bias: Seeing oneself as cause and target of others' behavior. *Journal of Personality*, *51*, 621–630.

Cambridge Elements ☰

Applied Social Psychology

Susan Clayton

College of Wooster, Ohio

Susan Clayton is a social psychologist at the College of Wooster
in Wooster, Ohio. Her research focuses on the human relationship with nature,
how it is socially constructed, and how it can be utilized to promote
environmental concern.

About the Series

Many social psychologists have used their research to understand
and address pressing social issues, from poverty and prejudice to work
and health. Each Element in this series reviews a particular area of applied
social psychology. Elements will also discuss applications of the research
findings and describe directions for future study.

Cambridge Elements ≡

Applied Social Psychology

Elements in the Series

Empathy and Concern with Negative Evaluation in Intergroup Relations:
Implications for Designing Effective Interventions
Jacquie D. Vorauer

A full series listing is available at: www.cambridge.org/EASP

Lightning Source UK Ltd.
Milton Keynes UK
UKHW020406150719
346128UK00011B/64/P